THE GOOD, THE BAD, AND THE UGLY
LOS ANGELES LAKERS

THE GOOD, THE BAD, AND THE UGLY
LOS ANGELES LAKERS

HEART-POUNDING, JAW-DROPPING, AND GUT-WRENCHING
MOMENTS FROM LOS ANGELES LAKERS HISTORY

Steven Travers

TRIUMPH
BOOKS

Triumph Books and colophon are registered trademarks of Random House, Inc.

Library of Congress Cataloging-in-Publication Data

Travers, Steven.
    The good, the bad, & the ugly Los Angeles Lakers / by Steven Travers.
        p. cm.
    Includes bibliographical references.
    ISBN-13: 978-1-60078-004-2
    ISBN-10: 1-60078-004-0
        1. Los Angeles Lakers (Basketball team)—History. 2. Basketball—History. I. Title. II. Title: Good, the bad and the ugly Los Angeles Lakers.

GV885.52.L65T73 2007
796.323'640979494—dc22

2007013220

This book is available in quantity at special discounts for your group or organization. For further information, contact:

Triumph Books
542 South Dearborn Street
Suite 750
Chicago, Illinois 60605
(312) 939-3330
Fax (312) 663-3557

Printed in U.S.A.
ISBN: 978-1-60078-004-2
Design by Patricia Frey
All photos courtesy of AP/Wide World Photos unless otherwise indicated.

To the biggest Lakers fans I know,
my wonderful cousins Bill and Jean Friedrichs.
And to two great friends,
the Cole brothers, Jeff and Brad.

CONTENTS

FOREWORD
A TRIBUTE TO ELGIN BAYLOR

Elgin Baylor was a man ahead of his time and ahead of the electronic age that turned athletes into television stars. He may be the greatest basketball player the modern world has ever known, perhaps the greatest basketball player ever.

Baylor was a 6'6", 225-pound package of grace, strength, and witticisms whose style prompted Chick Hearn to coin the phrase "Yo-yo-ing the dribble." Baylor took a game played on hardwood floors and lifted it to the heavens, from which it has never come down. His protégés were every high flyer from Dr. J to Michael Jordan to Kobe Bryant to LeBron James, stars whose moves and faces have inundated a nation obsessed with the visual.

The first pick by the then–Minneapolis Lakers in the 1958 draft, Baylor was persuaded to forego his senior year after taking Seattle University to the NCAA title game virtually by himself. "If he had turned me down," said team owner Bob Short, who a couple of years later would shift the Lakers to Los Angeles, "I'd have been out of business. The club would have gone bankrupt."

Instead it went into ascendancy, becoming the favorite team of the entertainment crowd. People were drawn by Baylor and a slender guard from West Virginia, Jerry West, whom Baylor nicknamed "Zeke from Cabin Creek"—a one-two billing that had Hollywood both envious and enthralled.

How good was Elgin Baylor? In his third season (1960–61), which was his first in Los Angeles, he averaged 34.8 points, 19.8 rebounds, and 5.1 assists per game.

How good was Elgin Baylor? "Pound for pound I think he was the best basketball player in the history of the game," said Tommy Hawkins, a onetime teammate who became a sports announcer and then a Dodgers executive.

How good was Elgin Baylor? In the 1980s, when Larry Bird was in his Celtics prime, onetime Celtic Tom Heinsohn was the color announcer for Boston games. Heinsohn was asked who the greatest forward was in the history of the game. His answer: Elgin Baylor.

In the early 1960s I was a young reporter with United Press International and then the [Santa Monica] *Evening Outlook,* both of which have now gone the way of the dodo bird. During my tenure as a reporter, I spent many hours at Lakers practices. Baylor would occasionally stand at the half-court circle and bet anyone foolish enough to accept that he could hurl balls back over his head into the basket 47 feet away. I saw him make three out of five one morning.

Baylor, in the army reserve, was called to active duty during the 1961 Berlin crisis. Allowed out of military uniform to suit up in a Lakers uniform, in the spring of 1962 he set a single-game Finals record that still stands, and which produced a lead paragraph for UPI that essentially read like this: "PFC Elgin Baylor, the Los Angeles Lakers' one-man army, scored 61 points against the Boston Celtics last night in Game 5 of the NBA Finals...."

Baylor was a creative offensive genius who gave birth to hang time and averaged more than 30 points a game during three seasons and more than 20 points a game during five other seasons. He could bull his way to the hoop or leap and toss in a smooth jumper.

He played in an era before the three-point basket became part of the sport and before the dunk became part of everyone's repertoire. More significantly, he played in an era before sports of any type became part of people's lives via the television.

Foreword

* * *

Steve Travers has written a book about the entire history of the Lakers, in Minneapolis and Los Angeles. The team has hosted many stars, but to my way of thinking, Baylor will always represent the kind of superstardom that marked this franchise. He was the template for all that followed. I still don't think he knows how good he really was.

—Art Spander

ACKNOWLEDGMENTS

Thanks to Tom Bast, Jess Paumier, Amy Reagan, Kelley White, Linc Wonham, and all the great folks at Triumph Books for having faith in me. Thanks also to Craig Wiley, as well as my literary manager, Peter Miller of PMA Literary and Film Management, Inc., in New York City. I want to thank the Los Angeles Lakers, a first-class organization, and Art Spander. Thanks to Karen Peterson for website support.

Of course, my thanks as always go out to my daughter, Elizabeth Travers; to my parents, Don and Inge Travers; and to my Lord and Savior, Jesus Christ, who has shed his grace on thee, and to whom all glory is due!

INTRODUCTION
A FABULOUS TEAM, A FABULOUS CITY, A "FABULOUS FORUM"

I fell in love with the Los Angeles Lakers at a young age. I loved their colors and their uniforms. I loved the "Fabulous Forum," which was the first of the truly great state-of-the-art basketball palaces. I loved the city they played in. The Lakers were fast, slick, and showy—perfect for Los Angeles.

In 1972 I was completely enamored with the Lakers. From my earliest beginnings, I was always interested in greatness. I enjoyed statistics, comparing the best teams and players of one era to another. In '72 the Lakers appeared to be the finest pro basketball team ever assembled.

They got off to a 4–0 start, and at first it seemed incongruous. For years, super-talented Lakers teams challenged seemingly less-talented Boston and New York squads, each time ending in resounding disappointment. The Jerry West saga was a national soap opera, a timeworn tragedy worthy of *Hamlet* or *Macbeth*.

With the Lakers at 6–3, the great Elgin Baylor was injured and announcing his retirement. If the Lakers of Baylor, West, and Wilt Chamberlain could not capture the NBA title, how could they hope to do it without their incredible superstar forward? They had a new coach, a martinet seemingly out of touch with the modern athlete. How could Bill Sharman motivate Chamberlain when so many others had failed?

They seemed to be a bluff. It was generally thought that this team would have trouble fending off the Golden State Warriors in their division, much less challenge the likes of defending champion Milwaukee for league supremacy. I remember watching the Bucks early that season. I had followed their superstar center, Lew Alcindor, since his days at UCLA. However, I did not see Alcindor's name in the daily line scores.

"Alcindor must be injured," I thought to myself. For several games I looked for Big Lew. No Alcindor.

"But who is this Jabbar guy?" I mused. "Where'd he play college ball? He's scoring 34 points a game!"

I eventually figured out that Alcindor had changed his name to Kareem Abdul-Jabbar. The season began to play itself out, and the Lakers started winning...and winning...

Sports Illustrated checked into it. Amazingly, they reported, "Wilt the Stilt," a notorious late riser, was willing to attend Sharman's early-morning "shoot-arounds" as long as the team got good results. The more the team won, the more willing Wilt was to rise and shine.

Los Angeles won 33 straight games. It was a modern professional sports record, one that has never been approached in all the years since. I had never seen a team play basketball like this. Then they traveled to Milwaukee, where Abdul-Jabbar and the Bucks ended the streak. But Los Angeles beat Golden State by an incredible 63 points en route to finishing 69–13, the best regular-season record ever. However, as all true Lakers fans knew, it meant nothing unless it was accompanied by ultimate victory in the NBA Finals.

The road to the Finals went through—you guessed it— Milwaukee, and the 7'2" Abdul-Jabbar was at the very height of his career. In Game 1, Milwaukee beat the Lakers at home as thoroughly as any team I have ever seen. It was a total drubbing, and it looked like "next year" was not this year, again.

Game 2 was a death struggle, with L.A. fighting like the 101st Airborne Division defending Bastogne in the Battle of the Bulge. The star of the game was not Chamberlain or West, but Jim McMillian, who went on a scoring rampage in the 135–134 thriller.

Form played itself out after that, with the Lakers overcoming a few more bumps before beating Milwaukee in six. After losing Game 1 to New York, they swept four straight to *finally* bring home the title. I will never forget the look on Jerry West's face. He did not play like a champion and did not look like a champion. He looked like one of those Airborne Rangers in Bastogne after George Patton's forces eventually rescued them from certain death. After years of heroic defeat, he was a survivor because his team had not let him down.

I was hooked. The Lakers became my team. And they have always remained my team.

IN THE CLUTCH

MR. CLUTCH

Jerry West was born in Chelyan, West Virginia, on May 28, 1938. West Virginia is coal country, a small state, poor. West, fighter ace Chuck Yeager, and legendary Southern California football coach John McKay are likely the three most famous personalities to emerge from this hardscrabble existence. All made their marks in—or in the skies above—California.

Chelyan is near a town called Cabin Creek, and while West was not actually from Cabin Creek, nevertheless his great teammate, Elgin Baylor, gave him the nickname "Zeke from Cabin Creek." That was his moniker in the 1960s, a time when he and Baylor were developing into pro basketball stars. But by the end of the decade, West's nickname, known far and wide, was "Mr. Clutch."

In the history of sports, there is nothing more revered than the ability to come through in the clutch. Some of the greatest athletes who ever lived have been derided for failing to do so; some rightly, some wrongly.

Ted Williams is thought to be the finest hitter in baseball history, but his lack of production in the 1946 World Series overshadowed his Triple Crowns and MVP awards for years.

Barry Bonds has been compared to Williams, but his postseason failures in Pittsburgh and the San Francisco Giants' inability to win the 2002 World Series—despite a superhuman effort by Bonds—dog his legacy.

Young fans might not remember, but Jerry West, a coal miner's son from West Virginia, was such a clutch player that it is a stretch to say any of the superstars that have come after him were any better.

On the other hand, San Francisco 49ers quarterback Joe Montana is considered the greatest of all signal callers, ahead of players with gaudier statistics and natural abilities, because he won "the big one" and shined in "the clutch."

Reggie Jackson is by no means the best hitter ever, but in the mind's eye "Mr. October" is a New York and Oakland icon because he did it when it counted. West's teammate, Wilt Chamberlain, on the other hand, suffered from a reputation for "clutching up," which is the worst malady an athlete can have.

Chamberlain may be the greatest physical specimen the hoops game has ever known. He was a marvelous athlete, a collegiate high jumper with speed, agility, seven-foot height, size, and Herculean strength. His rival, Bill Russell of the Boston Celtics, was a relatively short man by comparison, thin, and lacking offensive prowess, but historians generally regard Russell as the greater of the two because of his star power when the game was on the line. Chamberlain, even though he won at Philadelphia a few years earlier, truly shed the monkey on his back when he and West won the 1972 championship.

When West retired in 1974, he was a 10-time First Team All-NBA selection. At that point, he and Oscar Robertson were unquestionably the two greatest guards in pro basketball history.

Since then, Michael Jordan and perhaps Magic Johnson are thought to be better, but despite the greatness of these two players, purists are resistant to the notion. West was simply so good, and so *clutch*, that it seems incongruous that anybody was ever better.

West and Robertson also represented a new wave of superstardom in the NBA. They were bigger and more athletic than their predecessors. Theirs was a jump-shot era, replacing the set-shot 1950s. West and Robertson ushered in a new age, changing the face of the game forever. Both were equally skilled in every facet of basketball. Their rivalry marks the game like that of the Chamberlain-Russell duels, or the Ted Williams–Joe DiMaggio baseball comparisons of an earlier time.

Had Jerry West been born much earlier, the world would not have known of him. His father was a poor coal mine electrician who struggled to meet the needs of his wife and five children. Jerry was the fourth child. When he was 12, his older brother David, serving in the armed forces, was killed in the Korean War.

"He was almost a perfect person," said West. "You would almost say to yourself, 'My goodness, why didn't it happen to me?' because this person was so good.... It changed me from being extremely aggressive to unbelievably passive, and maybe more introverted than I should have been at that point in my life."

West's father nailed a hoop to a shed outside a neighbor's house. In the winter, spring, summer, and fall, West practiced on the dirt-covered court. When the weather got cold, he wore gloves. He played and played and played, missing meals, shooting until his fingers bled. He shot well into the night, practicing by the light of the moon. He became malnourished and required medical treatment.

His desire was spurred by his failure to make the junior high school team. In his junior year at East Bank High, West made varsity but played sporadically. In the summer between his junior and senior years, West grew to six feet in height. As a senior he blossomed, averaging 32 points per game. West was the best prep basketball player in the state, the first player in West Virginia history to score 900 points in a single season. East Bank claimed the 1956 state title. So great was West that East Bank was renamed West Bank for a day, a tradition carried on each March 24 (the anniversary of the championship game his senior year). While the town changed its name only once a year, the high school made it permanent: West Bank High School.

More than 60 colleges courted West's services. The game was growing by leaps and bounds. It was a popular Olympic sport (dominated by the Americans) and considered a "city game" that blended white and African American players in seamless team play. Russell's University of San Francisco Dons were a dynasty of the collegiate game, but Southern California, UCLA, and California on the West Coast; Kentucky and North Carolina in the South; and Kansas in the Midwest had top programs.

West stayed local, choosing the West Virginia Mountaineers, where he was a two-time All-American, averaging almost 25 points per game. In a game against legendary coach Adolph Rupp and the Kentucky Wildcats, West broke his nose in the first half. Hardly able to breathe, he returned to the lineup in the second half with gauze stuffed in his bleeding nostrils. His 19 points spurred the Mountaineers to an upset over Kentucky.

In 1959 West led West Virginia to the NCAA championship game. He scored 28 points in a losing effort, 71–70 against California and their legendary coach, Pete Newell. Newell would later become an integral member of the Lakers organization.

In five 1959 NCAA playoff games, West led his team in scoring and rebounding, tying the tournament record with 160 points. Despite great accolades accorded West, showcasing his talents for the first time on a national basis, he was inconsolable after the one-point loss to the Golden Bears.

"He hated losing more than any man I've ever been around in my life," said Pat Riley, who later became a teammate and coach of the Lakers. West was utterly single-minded about victory, which meant that he was not able to enjoy his career nearly as much as other stars. Instead of looking forward to games, he was miserable, physically ill, a bundle of nerves. Defeats, of course, gnawed at him, removing any joy a normal player might otherwise derive from scoring 30 points a night. Victories were never enough—he wanted more. Another game to win, another challenge to meet, another mountain to climb.

His career, almost ironically, was filled with as much disappointment as any player of his era, if not ever. Over time, his angst became so publicly known that the fans, the entire country, agonized with Jerry. When ultimate victory finally did come his way in 1972, the look on his face and his demeanor more closely resembled a man let out of prison than the winner of a sporting event.

West was a total perfectionist. Lakers wins did not satisfy him unless he felt he had played perfectly. Games that pundits judged

SCANDAL

In the summer of 2003, Kobe Bryant had it all: fame, fortune, youth, looks, and a beautiful wife. But just as Camelot came to its mythological end when the king's most trusted knight had an affair with his wife, so too did the Lakers version of Camelot find a symbolic conclusion. Kobe went to a Colorado spa for relaxation and hooked up with a young blonde employee of the spa. Something happened; exactly what has never really been explained. The girl yelled *rape*. Kobe claimed the sex was consensual, which was a tough pill to swallow for his wife, but, considering the lifestyles of professional athletes, not exactly the greatest surprise. Many argued that the girl was looking for a payoff, notoriety, or both. In the end, the case was dismissed, but the ordeal stained Kobe's almost immaculate reputation.

to be perfect were more often than not considered below the standards West set for himself.

In 1960, the two marquee college players were West and Cincinnati's Oscar Robertson. Robertson was a confident player who relished the opportunity to display his considerable skills. West didn't think he was good enough to play in the National Basketball Association, but the Lakers did not share his doubts.

The Cincinnati Royals selected Robertson as a "territorial player." The league reserved the right for teams to pick players from their geographical region in order to build up a fan base, but the Royals already had the first overall pick and would have selected Robertson in any event. West was hoping to go to the New York Knickerbockers with the third pick, but the Minneapolis Lakers then selected him with the second pick. West was disappointed, but shortly after the draft Minneapolis announced that they were moving to Los Angeles, a move that seemed daunting and also exciting to the young West Virginian.

Before signing a $15,000 contract, however, West teamed up with Robertson to play for the U.S. Olympic team in the Rome Summer Games. The 1960 American team was considered for decades to be the finest amateur team ever assembled. Ten of its players went on to star in the NBA. The United States won eight Olympic games by an average of 42 points. West returned home with the gold medal.

The sights and sounds of burgeoning Los Angeles astounded the country boy. The Lakers helped ease the transition for him by bringing in his West Virginia coach, Fred Schaus, to take over the team. Schaus considered West the "perfect" guard, the "man that has everything. A fine shooting touch, speed, quickness, all the physical assets, including a tremendous dedication to the game."

Despite Schaus's fatherly presence, West considered the 1960–61 season at the Los Angeles Sports Arena to be "the worst year of my life in basketball." The Lakers were coming off a 25–50 record. The team failed to mesh in the first half of the season. In the second half of the year, West and Elgin Baylor, another young star recently drafted off the campus of Seattle University, began to display their great abilities in a way that turned Los Angeles around.

West averaged 17.6 points per game. Baylor flowered into a superstar, scoring almost 35 points per game. The West-Baylor combination became the greatest the game had ever seen. Los Angeles improved to a second-place finish in the NBA West, then extended a favored Hawks team to seven games in the Western Division Finals. The veteran Hawks pulled out the final two games by a total of three points to advance.

Baylor missed most of the 1961–62 season due to military service, so West, fully developed by now, raised his game and his scoring average to new levels (30.8 per game). On January 17, playing with a bandage on his nose, he scored 63 points against the Knickerbockers, then the record for a guard. He powered 31.5 points per game in the postseason, elevating Los Angeles to the NBA Finals before succumbing to the mighty Boston Celtics.

In the third game of the Finals, West sank two jump shots in the last minute of the game to tie it up. With three seconds on the clock, "Mr. Clutch" intercepted a pass from Boston's Sam Jones and scored the winning layup in L.A.'s 117–115 victory.

"I've never forgotten it," said West. "Everyone wants to hit a home run in the ninth inning to win the big game. That was my home run."

Despite his heroics, the 1962 series with Boston was a portent of great 1960s frustration for West, the man who despised losing but did not know how to enjoy winning. Los Angeles forged a three games to two lead, but the great Celtics tied it up with a Game 6 win. In the penultimate game, the game was tied at an excruciating 100–100. Lakers guard Frank Selvy shot one from 15 feet with time running out, but it bounced off the rim. In overtime, Boston earned their fourth straight NBA title by outscoring the Lakers 10–7 to win the game, 110–107. West was a gentleman in defeat, but the loss was a source of "unbelievable frustration" to him.

The following year an injury sidelined West for 27 games, but when he returned he was able to spur his team to another Western Division championship. The road to West's destiny as a champion again led through Boston. This time, it was even closer. While Boston won it in six games instead of seven, their four wins were by an average of only four points.

It was always something for the Lakers in this star-crossed decade. They were the toasts of Los Angeles, a glamour team in Hollywood. However, just as West's 1962–63 season was marred by his leg injury, in 1964–65 the Lakers—the most talented team in the NBA—were set back by Baylor's severe leg injury in Game 1 of the Western Division finals versus the Bullets.

With Baylor on the sidelines, West took the team on his shoulders like the heroic character in Ayn Rand's *Atlas Shrugged*. West scored 49 points to key the 121–115 win over the Bullets and followed that up with a 52-point effort in the Game 2 victory. The Bullets won the next two games to even the series at two, but West scored 44 and 48 points in those two defeats. In Games 5 and 6, West scored 43 and 42 points, respectively, keying two wins and sending Los Angeles back to Boston.

In the Bullets series, West averaged an incredible 46.3 points per game, a playoff series record that has never been topped. He scored 40 points or more in a record six straight playoff games.

But the loss of Baylor was too much against the healthy, veteran, champion Celtics. West scored 34 points a game versus Boston, but it was not enough. The Celtics won it in five. West's playoff scoring average was 40.6. In 1965–66, Boston dashed Los Angeles's hopes again, squeaking out a two-point win in a seventh game that left West exasperated beyond belief.

In 1966–67, Wilt Chamberlain and the Philadelphia 76ers fashioned a monster season, featuring an NBA-record 68 regular-season wins and the world championship, but in 1967–68 it was

WINNERS

Karl Malone, one of basketball's all-time greats, played one year in Los Angeles. In 2003–04 he teamed with Kobe and Shaq, helping to lead Los Angeles to the Finals before they lost in five games to Detroit.

again Boston versus Los Angeles. By
this time, the Lakers were playing at
the "Fabulous Forum." They were a
team of stars while the Celtics
appeared old, but West's team could
not get over the hump. Boston
knocked them off in six games. The
next year, Chamberlain was brought
over from Philadelphia.

Surely their time had come.
Chamberlain was the most domi-

DID YOU KNOW...

That the 1972 All-Star
Game was played at the
Forum? Jerry West was
named MVP as the West
won. Wilt Chamberlain also
starred in that game.

nant basketball player ever, and possibly the most dominant athlete
since Babe Ruth. Baylor was healthy, a star at the height of his game,
as was West. Nothing could stop such a team, except for the fact that
the term *team* had to be applied loosely to these Lakers. Egos,
salaries, and L.A. star power seemed to overshadow their on-court
chemistry. In 1969, Bill Russell, now operating as player-coach of the
aging Celtics, was able to take a team that finished fourth in their
division during the regular season to the NBA title. In the seventh
and final game, Boston eked out a two-point win over the Lakers.
West enjoyed zero consolation over becoming the only player to win
the Most Valuable Player award in a losing Finals.

Of all of West's disappointing seasons, however, the 1969–70
campaign may have been his most frustrating. Under Coach Joe
Mullaney, who took over from Butch van Breda Kolff, the superstar Lakers struggled to a 46-win regular season but entered the
playoffs with high hopes. With Russell retired, Boston was a complete nonfactor in 1970. However, the vacuum of power was filled
by the Knickerbockers.

For years an also-ran in the NBA, the 1969–70 Knicks under
coach Red Holzman thrilled crowds at Madison Square Garden
with a magical season. Led by center Willis Reed, guard Walt
Frazier, and forward "Dollar Bill" Bradley, they were the toasts of
the Big Apple.

Los Angeles seemed to fight themselves as much as the
opposition, struggling to make it past the expansion Phoenix
Suns in seven games before winning four straight from Atlanta.

A dream matchup between teams from L.A. and New York was on when the Knicks survived Lew Alcindor and Milwaukee in the East.

The teams split the first two, setting up a memorable Game 3 that captured the essence of West's career. The score was 100–100 at the Fabulous Forum when Knicks forward Dave DeBusschere hit what looked to be the winning shot with three seconds left. Chamberlain threw the in-bounds pass to West, who heaved a desperation 60-footer that sailed through the net with air to spare, sending the game into overtime.

It may have been West's greatest moment. It certainly sealed his Mr. Clutch reputation. At the time it was worth only two points, instead of the winning three that it would be today.

"The man's crazy," Knicks guard Walt Frazier recalled thinking when he saw West eyeing the long shot. "He looks determined. He thinks it's really going in."

West's melancholy career was marked by the fact that, despite one of the best—if not *the* best—clutch shots in league history occurring with everything on the line in a venerable New York setting, his team failed to capitalize on it. They lost in overtime, 111–108. West had 34 points and nine assists. The press crowded around his locker afterward, but he had no desire to accept the slightest glory.

"It doesn't really matter, does it?" he said. "Because we lost."

That was not the end of the series, however. West pushed and prodded his team all the way to a seventh game. Reed injured his thigh and seemed unable to play, meaning that Los Angeles had an enormous advantage in the last game. Reed stoked Madison Square Garden cheers by hobbling onto the floor, but he was basically ineffective, at least from an offensive standpoint, because of the pain he was in.

With a chance to dominate in his usual manner, Chamberlain instead seemed to give up, to the astonishment of fans, media, teammates, and opponents. In the end it cost West and the Lakers their best shot ever at the NBA title.

The next year, more disappointment had West thinking seriously about retirement. Like baseball's Ernie Banks of the Chicago

PAIN AND SUFFERING

Five Saddest Days in Lakers History
- Magic Johnson announces he is HIV-positive.
- Game 7 of the 1969 Finals; Lakers lose to Boston with Wilt Chamberlain sitting on the bench.
- Game 4 of the 1984 Finals; Lakers blow a five-point lead with less than a minute left instead of going up 3–1.
- Chick Hearn passes away in 2002.
- Elgin Baylor is forced to retire just as the Lakers are about to start a 33-game winning streak in 1971.

Cubs, he was a beloved superstar who never won the big one, by no fault of his own. In 1970–71, Alcindor was joined by Robertson, who captured his first NBA title when he and Lew powered the Bucks all the way.

There was little indication that 1971–72 would be the Lakers' year. The championship road would have to be traveled through Milwaukee, which was now in the Western Conference. The Bucks were the elite team in the league. Los Angeles seemed over the hill. West had suffered assorted injuries and broken bones, all taking their toll on his 33-year-old body. His nose had been broken eight times. Baylor was hoping to play one last season, but it was not to be.

The salaries in basketball were starting to escalate rapidly. Chamberlain for one was living like a movie star in the Hollywood Hills, setting new standards for bachelorhood and a diva-like attitude toward his coaches and teammates. None of this was a recipe for success.

A succession of coaches with terrific pedigrees had failed to convert Wilt's great talent into a championship for Los Angeles. The new man, Bill Sharman, did not appear to be a good candidate for achieving this end. Sharman had been a terrific baseball and basketball star at the University of Southern California who sat on the Brooklyn Dodgers bench the day Bobby Thomson hit

11

the "Shot Heard 'Round the World" in 1951. He then went on to a Hall of Fame career with the Celtics.

He turned down the job at his alma mater, USC, and coached with success in the American Basketball Association. In 1971 he took over a Lakers team consisting entirely of individuals. He planned to use old-school methods to turn them into a team. At first it looked to be an impossible goal.

Sharman ordered morning practices on game days in order to get his team acclimated to the arenas. Chamberlain, a notorious late riser, had to be convinced of the wisdom of such a thing. A 33-game winning streak provided the evidence "Wilt the Stilt" needed. It was, and remains to this day, the longest winning streak in professional sports history.

For the first time ever, West did not have to carry the team on his back. Neither did Chamberlain. Gail Goodrich from UCLA was a scoring machine on a team that reached 100 points in 81 of 82 games without any single dominant offensive player. Both West and Chamberlain were happy to concentrate on playing great defense (both were masters) while dishing out assists.

Their 69–13 mark broke the 68–13 record of Chamberlain's 1967 Sixers champions. Chicago fell in four straight, but Karccm Abdul-Jabbar (the former Alcindor) and Milwaukee—the team that had ended the 33-game winning streak in January—posed the kind of formidable challenge that the Lakers had consistently failed to overcome over the previous decade.

In the opener, Milwaukee destroyed Los Angeles. It looked bleak, but the Lakers rallied to win in six games. A first-game loss to New York rekindled bad memories from 1970, but West's team

THE BEST OF TIMES, THE WORST OF TIMES, AND OVERTIMES

Game 3 of the 1970 NBA Finals between Los Angeles and New York was both the best and the worst of the team's overtime games. Jerry West's 63-foot shot as the buzzer sounded forced the extra period. In that extra period the Lakers lost. It symbolized the team's and Jerry's 1960s-era frustration.

was too good. They won four straight to capture their first NBA title on the West Coast.

The TV cameras entered the Lakers dressing room at the Forum, and of course West was asked how great it all was. He did not look particularly happy. He smiled, but rather like a man who had seen too much war to really celebrate peace.

"You've heard that song, 'Is That All There Is?'" he said. "That's pretty much how I felt. It still never, even to this day, will replace the pain of those other losses."

West retired as the third-highest scorer in league history. He felt that he could still play, but not up to his demanding standards. In 1973 the Lakers made it back to the Finals, only to lose to New York, so it was more frustration for West to deal with.

West was named to the All-Defensive Team four times in the first five years the team was chosen. Jordan, Robertson, and Johnson may have been arguably better all-around players, but West's defensive acumen was better than any of them. It was his clutch shooting, however, that forged his legacy.

"He was undoubtedly the greatest shooter when the game was on the line," said Sharman. "Throughout his career, he must have won 40 to 50 games with the last basket."

In 1979 West was elected to the Naismith Memorial Basketball Hall of Fame. In 1976 he was hired to replace Sharman as the team's coach. In three years he compiled a 145–101 record, making the playoffs each year. When Jerry Buss bought the team, West moved to the front office, and in 1982 he became the general manager. He oversaw the great Showtime run of the 1980s and steered the team through the eras. A superb judge of talent, West signed Shaquille O'Neal away from the Orlando Magic, and he made the key decision to draft Kobe Bryant in 1996.

"The average person wouldn't understand the pressure and stress that I've felt in my life," he said before announcing his retirement in 2000. "I need to get off this merry-go-round for a while."

"The greatest honor a man can have," said Bill Russell on Jerry West Night in 1971, "is the respect and friendship of his peers. You have that more than any man I know."

The silhouette on the NBA logo is, naturally, Jerry West driving to the basket.

MAN-CHILD

If ever a guy looked to have been born and bred to play pro basketball, it was Kobe Bryant. His father, Joe "Jelly Bean" Bryant, played eight seasons in the NBA as well as in the Italian pro leagues. Bryant spent part of his childhood in Italy, learning the language so well that at one point it became his native tongue.

At Lower Merion High School in Pennsylvania, Bryant's 2,883 points made him the highest scorer in southeastern state history, surpassing records set by Wilt Chamberlain of Philadelphia Overbrook. He was named the national Player of the Year after leading Lower Merion to the state championship, after which he became the 27th player to make the jump from the preps to the pros. He was the first high schooler ever taken by Los Angeles.

In 1996–97 he learned the ropes, displaying brilliance enough to convince most that the risky move of skipping college was, in his case at least, the right move. In Bryant's second year, his 15.4 points per game were the most of any nonstarter in the NBA. In 1998–99 he averaged 20 points in the strike-abbreviated season.

But in 1999–2000, he came into his own. The "little brother" to Shaq O'Neal's "big brother," he averaged 22.5 points and five assists per game, registering 12 double-doubles. He converted a key game-winning basket in L.A.'s playoff win over Phoenix as the Lakers cruised to the NBA title.

In 2000–01 it appeared that Kobe was taking over for Shaq, at least in terms of scoring numbers. He averaged 28.5 points per game, scored 48 in a playoff game versus Sacramento, and helped L.A. to a repeat title.

The following year Bryant scored 25 points a game and was named MVP of the All-Star Game. The Lakers captured their third-straight NBA championship. Bryant and O'Neal had reached rarified air. The media picked up on little arguments between them, but Phil Jackson kept things running smoothly as he performed some of his best coaching work.

Signing with the Lakers out of high school and becoming a superstar and world champion in Los Angeles, Kobe Bryant is living a 21st-century version of the American Dream.

In 2002–03 Bryant was All-NBA and All-Defensive First Team, scoring 30 points a game, but this time San Antonio knocked off Los Angeles in the playoffs. After O'Neal departed for Miami, the Lakers became Kobe's team. He demonstrated Jordan-like scoring ability. In 2005–06 he averaged 35.4 points per game.

Bryant has reached superstar status in the NBA, living in a Newport Beach mansion. But with fame and money come problems. His marriage was rocked by the scandal of the 2003 rape allegations. Dealing with the media has been a learning process for him. He is extremely intelligent and savvy, and while his recent openness in the granting of interviews has been seen by some as a cynical ploy, others see it as a sign of maturity.

On January 22, 2006, Bryant scored 81 points in a 122–104 victory over the Raptors. Only Chamberlain, with 100 points, has scored more in a single NBA game.

"A hundred's not possible," Kobe told John Salley on *Best Damn Sports Show Period*. "Eighty-one was…I never felt like that in my life. I can't see that happening again."

ORIGINS

LAND OF 10,000 LAKES

Like most everything in California, the Lakers started someplace else. The only original professional sports franchise in the state is the San Francisco 49ers, which started in the fledgling All-American Football Conference after World War II.

The Rams came from Cleveland. The Dodgers and Giants of course were in New York, the A's in Philadelphia, then Kansas City. Expansion teams like the Angels and Padres were spawned from the success of Pacific Coast League teams. Hockey clubs like the Kings, Sharks, and Mighty Ducks are like trendy restaurants that open franchises in the suburbs. Basketball teams following the Lakers simply hoped to walk in their footsteps.

When it came to original sports teams in California, there were the minor leagues and the colleges. Both types were highly successful, whether it be the Los Angeles Angels and San Francisco Seals of the old PCL or major football powers at USC and California.

In Los Angeles, enormous crowds flocked to the Los Angeles Memorial Coliseum to watch Southern California, UCLA, and the Rams do battle. The USC Trojans were a postwar basketball powerhouse led by future Hall of Famers Alex Hannum and Bill Sharman, plus a third who should be, Tex Winter. Trojans coach Sam Barry was credited with inventing the "triangle offense," which he later taught to Phil Jackson in Chicago and of course to the Lakers.

UCLA emerged as a big-time basketball program under John Wooden in the 1950s, but by decade's end the perception was that Los Angeles was not a "basketball town." The weather was too perfect, the fans too interested in outdoor recreation to be cooped up in a sweaty gym. Indeed, the gyms *were* sweaty. USC played in a decrepit building that was seemingly called the "old gym" the day it was built. UCLA's basketball situation was even worse. They had a poor excuse for an arena known as the "B.O. Barn" for obvious reasons. When not playing at the "B.O. Barn," the Bruins were forced to play at a local high school or at Santa Monica City College.

John Wooden had been hired under the proviso that a state-of-the-art arena would be built on campus, but by 1960 he was still waiting with little promise that it would ever happen. But across town, next to the Coliseum across the street from USC, the L.A. Memorial Sports Arena was erected in 1959. It would be home to the Trojans until 2006. The Bruins would win two national championships playing there before Pauley Pavilion's 1965 opening.

The Sports Arena filled many needs in Los Angeles, not the least of which was as a convention hall. In 1960 the Democrats

SCHOOL TIES

USC and the Lakers have a major connection. From 1960 to 1967 they shared the L.A. Sports Arena. Coaches Bill Sharman and Tex Winter are Trojans. Owner Jerry Buss, his son Jim (vice president of player personnel), and his daughter Jeannie (executive vice president of business operations) are all USC alums. USC's Song Girls inspired the Laker Girls, and the first group literally consisted of alumni from the USC and UCLA dance teams. Entering the 2006–07 season, USC was tied for 10th among all colleges producing players on their roster over the years. This includes John Block, Mack Calvin, Duane Cooper, Bill Hewitt, and Cliff Robinson. UCLA with 15 (including Kareem Abdul-Jabbar, Keith Erickson, Gail Goodrich, Walt Hazzard, and Jamaal Wilkes) are by far number one.

nominated John F. Kennedy, and he gave his acceptance speech there. It would also be a major selling point in bringing the second Olympics to Los Angeles 25 years after its opening.

The Sports Arena—and this is not a joke—was considered one of the finest, if not the finest, basketball facilities in the country in the 1960s. Its opening meant that professional basketball could now come to the West Coast and its marquee city, Los Angeles.

The Minneapolis Lakers had once been an NBA dynasty, but the team suffered on the court and at the box office in the late 1950s. Ultimately Boston dominated the decade. When the Lakers moved from Minnesota to California in 1960, it ended a period of growth in the state and in pro basketball.

Minnesota was football country. The University of Minnesota Golden Gophers won three national championships in a row from 1934 through 1936 (no team has even won the Associated Press poll, which started in '36, three times straight). But there were no Twins, no Vikings. Those teams came into being, however, in part because of the popularity—albeit the star-crossed popularity—of the Minneapolis Lakers.

A local sportswriter named Sid Hartman came up with the name "Lakers," named after a ship that traversed the "Land of 10,000 Lakes." Hartman talked businessman Benjamin J. Berger into promoting a local exhibition game between Oshkosh and Sheboygan, two clubs in the National Basketball League (NBL). Established in 1937, it was a pro league in the Midwest. When 5,000 fans arrived for the game, Berger and Hartman knew they were on to something.

At the time, the NBL's Detroit Gems were in financial trouble after a 4–40 year. The team was in receivership, with its players shipped off to its competitors. Berger and promoter Morris Chalfen raised $15,000 and sent Hartman to Detroit to purchase the Gems from owner Winston Morris in 1947.

Max Winter was hired as general manager. Former local star John Kundla was brought on to coach the team. The early Lakers were an extension of the University of Minnesota's program. A big catch was Stanford All-American Jim Pollard. Pollard had been playing AAU ball for two years. But the man who would make the team a success was George Mikan.

In the late 1930s and early 1940s, Stanford's Hank Luisetti was thought to be the best player in the world. Luisetti is credited with "inventing" the jump shot. After World War II, a new breed of big man came to dominate the game. For many years, height was considered both a blessing and a curse in basketball. Tall players were too often immobile, unathletic, and clumsy—unable to take advantage of their natural edge.

Mikan was 6'10" tall but fully coordinated. He dominated at DePaul University in Chicago, so he was an enormous draw in

The first dominant big man, George Mikan, put the Lakers on the map when they first started playing basketball in Minneapolis in the late 1940s.

the Midwest. In 1946 Mikan signed with the NBL's Chicago American Gears, leading the team to the 1946–47 championship in his first season. After the season ended, Gears' owner Maurice White pulled his team out of the league. White had grandiose ideas: a 24-team league, financed by him, with the Gears as the centerpiece. He wanted to call it the Professional Basketball League of America, and in Mikan he saw the star who would anchor its success.

White's vision went up in flames, just as in baseball a new Mexican League, which had tried to entice stars like Ted Williams into going south of the border, had failed around that same time. When the Pro Basketball League of America folded, the Gears were broken up. Their players were distributed among the remaining teams. Mikan was easily the best player available, and, purely through chance, he became a Laker.

A dynasty was born. Bill Russell was entering junior high school, and in the years before he and the Celtics were the dominant force of the pro game, the Lakers and George Mikan were the best team in the game. In Mikan's first year with Minneapolis the team was 43–17, entertaining crowds at the Minneapolis Auditorium. In the best-of-five league championship finals, the Lakers defeated the Rochester Royals and ended the year winning the World Professional Tournament.

It was at this time that the Basketball Association of America was forming, with franchises in large eastern cities. They had completed their second season and had money, good marketing, and prime cities in their favor. The NBL had the better players. BAA president Maurice Podoloff, who got four NBL teams to jump to the BAA, sought a merger.

On May 10, 1948, the Lakers, Fort Wayne Pistons, Indianapolis Kautskys, and Rochester Royals paid a $25,000 entry fee to join the BAA. The suspicion that Mikan was the best player in the country and that his former league was the more talented was confirmed that first year. Mikan dominated 1948–49 play. In December of that season, Mikan scored 47 points against the Chicago Stags. He scored 53 against Baltimore. Scoring became all the rage in the league, with Joe Fulks of the Philadelphia Warriors getting 63 in a game with Indianapolis. At season's end, Mikan's 1,698 points were a new league record.

The NBL, however, was in trouble financially. The next year a merger was effectuated, with a 17-team organization coming into existence under the name of the National Basketball Association. That year the Lakers brought in guards Slater Martin and Bob Harrison, and forward Vern Mikkelsen. The 6'7" Mikkelsen might be considered the league's first power forward. Minneapolis won their regular-season title and then defeated Syracuse in a difficult six-game Finals to capture the NBA championship.

After an off year, they regained their footing and took three more NBA titles consecutively. Overall, they were champions in six of seven years.

"Standing shoulder to shoulder, Mikan, Mikkelsen, and Pollard looked like a ragged row of mountains," wrote sportswriter John Devaney.

The Lakers also played a series of entertaining barnstorming exhibition games with the popular Harlem Globetrotters. At that time the Globetrotters were still a serious team, unlike the more entertainment-based group they later became. Between 1948 and 1952, the Globetrotters and Lakers matched evenly in these games. By the mid-1950s, Globetrotters owner Abe Saperstein began to emphasize entertainment over competitiveness, which kept the 'Trotters successful for decades.

Mikan was so dominant that the league experimented by raising the height of the basket. The assessment after this ill-fated

WINNERS

Bill Sharman is the only coach to win the championship in all three major professional basketball leagues. His Cleveland Pipers won the American Basketball League title in 1961; the Utah Stars won the American Basketball Association championship in 1971; and the Lakers captured the 1972 NBA ring.

MIKAN "RULES"

George Mikan was so dominant that he inspired institution of the 24-second shot clock in 1954.

effort was that the higher basket "hurt the little fellow more than the tall one," wrote Dick Cullum in the *Minneapolis Tribune*.

"It didn't help the smaller guy," recalled Mikkelsen. "It helped me—the big, strong rebounder—because it gave me another tenth of a second to get set after a shot."

As happens with so many big men, Mikan was hacked, double-covered, and fouled constantly (many that were not called). It became frustrating for him, and after the 1954 season he retired. Mikan's departure was impossible for the club to overcome. They were competitive for a little while until Pollard quit. Mikan made a brief return, but the team faltered in the years in which Bill Russell and the Boston Celtics established their dominance of the NBA.

Attendance at Minneapolis Auditorium dipped. Conflicting events forced the team to sometimes play in alternative venues. Owner Ben Berger contemplated selling the club to Milton Fischman and ex–baseball star Marty Marion, who planned to make a move to Kansas City.

Enter Bob Short, a trucking executive who formed a large ownership group. Short's company, the Mueller Transit Company, helped purchase the Lakers for $150,000. They played in Minneapolis in 1958 but finished last. By so doing, they selected first in the draft, choosing Elgin Baylor from Seattle University.

Baylor sparked improvement, and the team made it to the NBA Finals before losing to Boston—the first of many such disappointments. In 1959–60, the Lakers were 25–50, but Short decided enough was enough. It was an era of expansion.

As far back as 1941, the St. Louis Browns were committed to moving to Los Angeles. Pearl Harbor canceled those plans. In the early 1950s, the Philadelphia A's and Boston Braves moved west, to Kansas City and Milwaukee, respectively.

In 1958 the Brooklyn Dodgers and New York Giants moved to California. The sound barrier had been broken in 1947. Commercial jet travel was now easily available to anybody, including sports teams. Bob Short saw the future in California.

The Dodgers' immediate success in Los Angeles, combined with enormous crowds watching USC, UCLA, and the Rams at the L.A. Memorial Coliseum, confirmed that there was enough interest for an expansion team that would come to be called the Angels. Short and insurance magnate Charlie O. Finley went after the franchise hard, but it was awarded to entertainer and radio executive Gene Autry.

However, the original Washington Senators moved into the new Metropolitan Stadium in Bloomington, Minnesota, and became the Minnesota Twins. That left the nation's capital without a baseball team. Short landed the second expansion team, also known as the Washington Senators. Short, who symbolizes the era of franchise shifts, eventually moved them to Texas, where they became the Rangers.

Things were looking good in Minneapolis, what with the new Twins and the expansion Vikings set to occupy Metropolitan Stadium in 1961. But interest in the baseball and football franchises left the basketball team, still without a true home arena, on the outside looking in. Short, having already explored Los Angeles as a baseball venue, moved the Lakers to L.A. for the 1960–61 season.

That was the beginning of the league's ascendancy. The Cincinnati Royals chose Oscar Robertson for the first pick in the draft. The Lakers chose Jerry West out of West Virginia. Just as the period 1979–80 marked the beginning of the Magic Johnson–Larry Bird rivalry, so too did 1960 mark the beginning of NBA greatness. The Celtics already had superstars like Bill Russell, K.C. Jones, and Bill Sharman, but few marquee names had emerged with other teams after Mikan's retirement.

In 1960, Ohio State won the NCAA championship with a team led by John Havlicek, Jerry Lucas, and Larry Siegfried. Their sixth man was Bobby Knight. In that year's Olympics, the United States dominated basketball competition. The game was modernizing, becoming popular, and now more thoroughly integrated.

Another superstar made his presence known: Wilt Chamberlain of the Philadelphia Warriors. Los Angeles represented Hollywood: glamour, wealth, and a new sense of style replacing the old ways. California, after all, had spawned the jump shot, supposedly invented by Hank Luisetti at Stanford.

Successful basketball teams had populated the West Coast for years. San Francisco, Stanford, and Cal all won national championships, as did Oregon State. The triangle offense was invented at USC. John Wooden, a pioneer when it came to providing opportunity to African American players at the collegiate level, was in the process of building a dynasty at UCLA. The time was ripe for the Lakers and pro basketball in Los Angeles.

THE TRIANGLE

Phil Jackson won six NBA championships in Chicago and three in Los Angeles. The hallmark of his success was the ballyhooed triangle offense. The triangle, as it turns out, was invented in Los Angeles. Two legendary basketball men with strong Lakers ties—Bill Sharman and Tex Winter—were there at the beginning.

It seems like it was only 60 years ago when these guys were basketball stars at the University of Southern California. That's right, USC. Before John Wooden turned Pauley Pavilion into Hoops Mecca, SC was a national power on the hardwood.

TRADING PLACES

In 1956, the Lakers made a trade with the Boston Celtics to secure Boston's number one pick in the draft. They wanted USF's Bill Russell. The papers were signed, but then Red Auerbach found out and forced the deal's termination. Because the Lakers and Celtics enjoyed "good relations," Los Angeles did not press the issue.

"The teams I played on," said Hall of Famer Bill Sharman (1947–50), "produced 19 NBA championship rings between myself, [Alex] Hannum, and Winter. Plus, we had Bob Kloppenberg, who coached in the pros."

The only other college that may have produced as many NBA titles would be the 1955–56 San Francisco Dons of Bill Russell and K.C. Jones. Considering Paul Westphal's success in Phoenix and Seattle, SC can lay claim to the top spawning ground of coaches this side of Dean Smith.

In the 1930s Tom McGarvin starred along with Gail Goodrich's father at USC. The game was much different then, not the run 'n' gun "Showtime" spectacle that it is today.

"They had nets around the court," said former East Coast basketball writer Jerry Cowle, "and players would bounce balls off them, playing the rebound."

That is why they were known as "cagers," but out west the "modern" game was being developed. Stanford's Hank Luisetti became basketball's first superstar, and legend has it that he invented the jump shot. Stanford won the national championship in 1942.

"Hank Luisetti, as far as I'm concerned," opined McGarvin, who played with Jackie Robinson at Pasadena's Muir High, "was the best player I ever saw during those years, but saying he invented the jump shot is a misnomer. Guys were using jump shots already. He did use one-handed shots more than anybody.

"We played at the Olympic Auditorium, the Shrine, the Pan-Pacific, anywhere we could find. I was the captain of the Trojan team that went to the Final Four and lost to Phog Allen and Kansas by one point in Kansas City. Everybody fouled out because the refs were Midwest homers, but we were as good as anybody."

Hamilton High's Hannum was a 6'7" enforcer who played with Sharman and Winter in 1946–47. Hannum's NBA career lasted until 1957. He went on to one of the most successful coaching careers of all time. Hannum led Wilt Chamberlain and the 1967 Philadelphia 76ers to the best record in NBA history (68–13; since broken by Sharman's '72 Lakers and the Phil Jackson–Winter Bulls of 1996). In 1969 he coached Rick Barry and the ABA's

The roots of basketball guru Tex Winter and his fabled triangle offense run deep in Los Angeles hoops lore.
Photo courtesy of Getty Images.

Oakland Oaks to that league's best-ever record (60–18). He was elected to the Hall of Fame in 1998.

The evolution of the triangle offense has an almost biblical quality to it. Doc Meanwell created it. His version begat Sam Barry, who begat Winter, who begat Jackson. Many have been disciples. Winter probably has done more to refine it than any coach.

"Barry picked it up from Doc Meanwell when he was a graduate student at Wisconsin," recalled Winter, who came to SC from Huntington Park and Compton College and has coached for well over half a century (including all six of Michael Jordan's championship teams and all three of the Jackson/O'Neal/Bryant champions).

FIGHTING MAD

Blackie Towery of the Ft. Wayne Pistons once punched Jim Pollard of the Lakers, knocking him into the seats. When Max Winter came to Pollard's defense, Towery punched him into the second row. In 1992, Towery called to apologize to Pollard. "You still mad at me?" he asked. Pollard laughed.

"Initially it was called the 'center opposite.' It was popularized on the West Coast by Jimmy Needles, and developed further by two Loyola players, Pete Newell and Phil Woolpert.

"It's based on 'reverse action,' and you don't want players with great individual skills who don't utilize the team game. That's what we're trying to teach Kobe Bryant," Winter said in 2000, when Bryant was still a very young player trying to stay in sync with the complicated system while playing his way out of Shaquille O'Neal's considerable shadow.

"It took Michael years to learn to play in the system. I try to teach them and let them know what's expected; ball control and player movement. Shaq O'Neal is so physically dominant that sometimes we get out of the system and just rely on him. Some better-skilled athletes are less effective in the Triangle."

Winter recalled the pre-Wooden UCLA rivalry.

"They had a great player named Don Barksdale," he said. "I recognized right off that Sharman was a great player. We had the 'buddy system,' where a younger player [Sharman] would be paired with a veteran [Winter]. Hannum was a leader and an enforcer."

"I was an All-American my last two years," said Sharman, who came to USC from Porterville after a year at Narbonne High in L.A. "We finished second my last three years, but beat UCLA when John Wooden was the coach. I was very impressed by Wooden immediately. He taught a fast-break style that was a big influence on my coaching career. I won four titles as a player with Boston, six as a coach, GM, and team president in the NBA.

"Jess Hill offered me the head coaching position at SC in the 1960s," Sharman recalled, "but the lack of an on-campus arena—a place where the students can get behind you, the team can practice—that plus I had pro offers, so I turned it down."

The Sports Arena was built in 1959, and while it was considered a great "on-campus" facility at the time (being across the street from the school), Pauley overshadowed it. The program was mired in mediocrity for years, but this "football school" can lay claim to three great coaching legends and an offensive style that was still in vogue in trendsetting L.A. more than half a century later.

VOICES

"HOT ROD" REMEMBERS THE LAKERS' FIRST YEAR

In 1960, the Democrats nominated JFK at the spanking-new Los Angeles Memorial Sports Arena. That was also the year the Lakers moved from Minneapolis to L.A., to play at the Sports Arena. Under the ownership of Bob Short, the team had experienced 12 successful years in the Midwest, jet travel had become a common event, while the Dodgers and Giants had recently led the way of Westward expansion. In their first year, the Lakers featured a rookie guard from West Virginia named Jerry West, who scored 17.6 points per game. They already had an established superstar, Elgin Baylor from Seattle University. Baylor scored an all-time franchise high 34.8 points per game that year, second in the NBA. He scored 71 on November 15 versus New York. The team was still finding themselves under coach Fred Schaus, going 36–43 for a second-place finish, but they managed to advance to the Western Division Finals before succumbing to a strong St. Louis team, 4–3. An integral member of those Lakers, the raucous Hot Rod Hundley, recalled the old Lakers and a simpler time.

L.A. Nostalgia

"I hung out with Bo Belinsky and Dean Chance at Ernie's House of Surface, at the 'Four Corners Where Friends Meet,' in Baldwin Hills," recalled Hundley. "We did the Sunset Strip all the time, the Whisky A-Go-Go, Gazzari's. The writers used to hang out at a

Hot Rod Hundley, winking for photographers during his college days at West Virginia in 1956, recalls a golden era in Los Angeles sports history. Photo courtesy of Bettmann/CORBIS.

restaurant on the Strip that I'd go to. I wasn't really into the bands. We also used to go to the La Marina Inn, a place at the beach in Marina del Rey. Everybody in the NBA went there, it was a good place to go in those days. I was good friends with Claude Crabbe of the Rams, and I used to go to a lot of Dodgers and Angels games. I loved being in L.A., it's still my favorite city. In my heart I would love to live in L.A. again. It's the greatest sports city in the world to me, and there's everything to do there; the beach, Hollywood, skiing, the lifestyle is casual and the fans are great. There's so many great sports teams, plus college sports with Southern Cal and UCLA, and schools like Pepperdine and Loyola. It's overcrowded, but nowadays every place is."

Bob Short

"Bob Short was great, a fabulous owner. One year we got beat in the seventh game Finals at Boston. Their pay for winning was $2,000, ours for finishing second was $1,000, which was a lot for us back then. So Short came in and said 'the toughest game is ahead of you,' meaning facing the press, then he said 'there's an extra thousand for each of you' so we'd make the same as Boston. Short did something that was like in a way not legal. We'd be down 20 at the half, he'd come into the locker room and he'd say 'here's $200' or 'here's $300,' if you win this game, or if you just played a good game. Once I left my billfold back in the hotel room, he just gave me a hundred and asked if that would be enough to get by. He'd just smile and do it in a way where I knew I wouldn't have to pay him back. He was Catholic, very straight-laced with nine kids or something, didn't drink, but he didn't condemn me for the way I lived. He was just amused by my carrying on."

Jim Murray
"He said West Virginia was the only state in America still on welfare."

Chick Hearn
"He said to me once, 'I hear you've been using all my lines,' and I said, 'Every one of 'em.' I'd love to replace Chick when he retires."

(Hearn passed away in 2002; Hundley, who conducted this interview in 2000, did not replace him.)

Elgin Baylor
"He was 'a ballet dancer in sneakers.' That was one of Murray's lines."

Wilt Chamberlain
"He had 78 points in a game against us, but we won, and 71 another time, but we won again. When he became a great all-around center his teams won."

Jerry West or Oscar Robertson?
"West was one of the five greatest players ever. The Big O would bitch at his teammates; he was so great but hard to get along with."

Bill Russell

"Bill Russell was quick like a cat, very smart and surrounded by greats like [John] Havlicek, [Frank] Ramsey, [Tom] Heinsohn, [Bob] Cousy, K.C., and Sam Jones, but he was the key, the difference was Russell. He was better than Chamberlain."

In *Tall Tales* by Terry Pluto, Hundley was quoted saying of Bob Cousy, "He was my idol...he scored 20 points on me in the first half. George Mikan was my coach and Mikan said, 'Hundley, I told you to watch Cousy, didn't I?'

"I said, 'I did, and he's great, isn't he?'"

CHICKIE BABY

It would seem a logical explanation that since Los Angeles is the entertainment capital of the world, L.A. sports teams have been blessed with the finest broadcasters. The town's media proximity, however, has little to do with the good fortune they have experienced. Vin Scully came to Los Angeles with the Dodgers when they arrived from Brooklyn.

Dick Enberg lived in Southern California and got his start announcing USC baseball games into a tape recorder before moving on to the Angels and then getting national gigs.

Bill King, like Scully, found himself in L.A. because his employer, the Raiders, moved there. Other great announcers have included Tom Kelly, Mike Walden, Ray Scott, Ross Porter, and Bob Miller.

When it comes to basketball, there is one name that stands out above all others: Chick Hearn. King, who did Warriors games for about two decades in addition to his football and baseball

MEDIA MONSTERS

When Chick Hearn, who dressed with respect for his profession, saw a particularly ruffled sportswriter he would say, "Aren't the lights working in your hotel room?"

work, drew raves and favorable comparisons with his Lakers counterpart. However, Chick's association with such a great team, his longevity, and his reputation as a basketball guy, not a multisport announcer, makes him the premier hoops voice of all time.

Some have mentioned Johnny Most of the Celtics, but that is even more of a joke than saying that Harry Caray, who was poorly prepared but made up for it with humor, was the best baseball voice. Sometimes Most would say something like, "Ball goes to number five. He finds the big fella inside, rebound by the redhead."

Hearn was prepared, professional, and absolutely paramount in terms of pure talent—his ability to discern the game and its intricacies, to describe in real time the fast pace of pro basketball, not with the brushstrokes of a French impressionist but with the detail of a Dutch master.

While Chick was totally associated with Lakers basketball, he in fact got his start announcing USC football in the 1950s. He took over as the voice of the Los Angeles Lakers with their first team of 1960–61. Between 1965 and 2001, Chick announced an incredible 3,338 consecutive Lakers games. Unlike some radio voices, Hearn was just as entertaining and descriptive on television.

Hearn was especially known for "Chickisms." According to www.Reference.com, the following phrases are attributed to Chick Hearn:

An "air ball" was a shot that draws nothing but air. "[He sent that one back] Airmail Special!" was a strongly blocked shot, often

TONGUE-TIED

Chick Hearn was a master interviewer, but he may have met his match during a Christmas Day game in Portland. A group of local kids were gathered for him to ask on the air how they were enjoying Christmas. The first little girl announced, "My family are atheists and don't celebrate Christmas." Hearn joked about the advance work on that interview for years.

Chick Hearn, the unmistakable voice of the Lakers for 3,338 consecutive games, easily ranks as one of the greatest sports announcers of all time.

sent high into the stands. *"Bloooows* the layup!" was a very easy missed layup. "Boo-birds" were fans who booed their own team when they played badly. "[He did the] bunny hop in the pea patch" was a player called for traveling. "[You could] call it with Braille" was an easy call for an official.

"[He got] caught with his hand in the cookie jar" was a reaching foul. The free throw line became the "Charity Stripe." Great defense had a team "covered like the rug on your floor." A bad team "couldn't beat the Sisters of Mercy." A poor shooting team "couldn't throw a pea into the ocean." A shot at the buzzer will "count if it goes... It *go-o-o-oes!"* (If the shot was successful.)

If a shot missed the rim but hit the backboard it "didn't draw iron." When the score was 10–5 it was a "dime-store score." He invented the terms "dribble-drive" and "finger roll." Wilt Chamberlain's blocked shots were "fly-swatted." A "football score" was 21–14, 38–35, and the like. His "frozen ropes" were picked up by baseball announcers describing line drives. He watched the games from "high above the western sideline."

A player dribbling the ball while doing a little hop step "hippity-hops the dribble." Hearn and former color commentator

Keith Erickson would bet each other an ice cream on a shot, a game, or some other outcome. The well-used term "he's got ice water in his veins" was a Chickism describing a player hitting a clutch free throw.

The end of a sloppy game was the now well-worn "garbage time." A "give and go" was when a player passed the ball, made a quick cut, and received a return pass. "[In and out], heart-*brrrreak!*" was a shot that appeared to go in, rattled around the rim, and missed. If it seemed to penetrate the basket before bounding out, Chick said, "You could read the commissioner's name from below."

"He has two chances, slim and none, and slim just left the building," was credited to Chick. "If that goes in, I'm walking home" was another way of saying, "He hasn't got a prayer." An off-balance shot was a "Leapin' Lena."

"[There are] lots of referees in the building, only three getting paid," he said when the crowd disagreed with a call. "The mustard's off the hot dog" was when a player attempted a bad shot resulting in a turnover. A close game was "nervous time." A basketball court was a "94-by-50 hunk of wood."

"No harm, no foul." Yes, a Chickism. So was "no blood, no ambulance, no stitches." A dumb play was "not Phi Beta Kappa." A long time since L.A. had the lead was "since Hector was a pup."

"He's in the popcorn machine [with butter and salt all over him]," was a famed description of a defensive player getting faked into the air by a pump fake.

"[He's] on him like a postage stamp" meant tight D.

"Slam dunk!" of course was a Chickism, courtesy of Wilt Chamberlain.

"[He] takes him to the third floor and leaves him at the mezzanine" was where an offensive player pump-faked a defender, drawing a foul. "Tattoo dribble" was dribbling the ball while not moving.

"This game's in the refrigerator: the door is closed, the lights are out, the eggs are cooling, the butter's getting hard, and the Jell-O's jigglin'!" was probably Chick's most famous phrase, used to describe a game when the outcome is secure.

RIVALRIES

The Lakers and Celtics are considered the greatest rivalry in the NBA, but if a rivalry is marked by competitiveness between the two teams, the 1960s were not a rivalry but rather Celtic domination (the Celtics won six Finals in the matchups, while the Lakers won zero).

A really bad shot was a "brick."

"Throws up a prayer (...*it's answered!*)" could describe Jerry West's 63-footer to tie the Knicks in the 1970 Finals. A bad foul call might be "ticky-tack." A player has achieved a "triple-double" with 10 or more in any three of these categories: points, rebounds, steals, assists, or blocked shots. A player taking a tumble on his behind fell "on his wallet." Listening to the broadcast on the radio was a "words-eye view." A gum chewer was "working on his Wrigley's" or had "stock in Wrigley's." Dribbling without movement was "yo-yoing."

Kareem Abdul-Jabbar was "Cap," "the Captain," or "Big Fella." He called Kobe Bryant "the Kid," Cedric Ceballos "Garbage Man," and Michael Cooper "Secretary of Defense." Rick Fox was "Foxy," and Gail Goodrich was "Stumpy" (although credit for that goes to Elgin Baylor, who also created West's moniker "Zeke from Cabin Creek").

Magic Johnson was "Buck." Shaquille O'Neal was another "Big Fella." He called Kurt Rambis "Blue-Collar Kurt" or "Clark Kent." James Worthy was "Big-Game James." Nick Van Exel was "Nick the Quick" and "Nick Van Excellent."

Sedale Threatt: "Thief of Baghdad."

Eddie Jones: "Fast Eddie" and "the Pickpocket."

Derek Fisher: "Fish."

Chick was uniquely L.A. in a breezy Southern California, old-school movie promoter kind of way.

"Chick was not one to hold a grudge," said Susan Stratton, his longtime producer on KCAL. "You would certainly know it when he was unhappy. If he liked you, he would call you 'Dum Dum.'

PATSIES

San Francisco and Los Angeles and the larger regions—Bay Area versus the Southland, NoCal versus SoCal—are natural rivals. The Giants and Dodgers are arguably the greatest historical rivalry in baseball, if not in all of sports. The 49ers and Rams had a terrific, fairly even rivalry until the 49ers became a dynasty and the Rams moved to St. Louis. The colleges get after it, too. But the Warriors (who played in San Francisco until 1971 and in Oakland ever since) have barely been a rival of the Lakers, going 105–172 against L.A. and winning only one NBA title. In 1972 the Lakers scored 162 points versus Golden State.

Then it all was forgiven. Our crews on the road loved him. He always noticed and acknowledged the people who worked with him on the broadcast."

Hearn was a practical joker who would get on the team bus, announcing that some player had been traded and causing great consternation until it was discovered to be a hoax. But he mixed it in with announcements of actual trades, so nobody ever quite had him figured out.

Wilt Chamberlain called him "Chickie Baby," a combination of endearment, respect, and a little bit of fear, because Hearn could make or break a player with the public if he wanted to.

After his 3,338th straight game, he had heart surgery, followed by other health problems, but returned to a standing ovation from a sellout crowd in 2002. A few months later, he passed away unexpectedly. Chick Hearn was a basketball poet.

WHEN THE FAT LADY SINGS

FRUSTRATION

The arrival of the Lakers in 1960 marks the beginning of a golden era in L.A. In 1961, the great Jim Murray began his column at the *Los Angeles Times*, which, more than any other factor, transformed the paper from partisan and provincial into a world-renowned publication.

A year later, the Dodgers moved into the greatest of all sports palaces, Dodger Stadium. John McKay turned the USC Trojans into a juggernaut. Across town at UCLA, John Wooden was about to do the same thing with the Bruins basketball program, which in turn led to the erection of Pauley Pavilion. The Rams were a popular pro football franchise packing huge crowds into the mammoth Coliseum.

Hollywood entered its greatest decade. Two Los Angeles political figures, Richard Nixon and Ronald Reagan, were in the process of standing astride the national stage. A city grew up, taking its rightful place alongside New York, Chicago, London, and Paris.

The Lakers of the 1960s were talented, exciting, and popular. For the first five years they played at the L.A. Sports Arena. The creation of this building gave Bob Short incentive to move his franchise from Minneapolis to Los Angeles. The Sports Arena eventually was criticized as a facility unworthy of USC or the Clippers, but when the Lakers played there it was, in fact, a modern arena and one of the finest in the nation by the standards of the day.

The image many have of the Lakers revolves around Jerry West, Elgin Baylor, and later Wilt Chamberlain playing at the "Fabulous Forum," but the early Lakers of the Sports Arena years were great teams. Unfortunately, this was the heyday of Bill Russell's Celtics. As good as Los Angeles was, Boston was always better.

In 1961–62, Los Angeles won the NBA's Western Division with an impressive 54–26 mark. They defeated the Detroit Pistons in the division finals, but Red Auerbach's Celtics bested them in a seven-game Finals. Lakers guard Frank Selvy's shot missed by inches, forcing overtime, which was won by Boston.

Between 1963 and 1968, Los Angeles lost four times in the Finals, always at the hands of Boston. In 1963 they were 53–27, good for first place in the Western Division. Coach Fred Schaus's team featured Baylor, second in the NBA with a 34-points-per-game average, followed by West with 27. Again, it was Boston in the Finals, and again the Celtics prevailed, this time in six games.

In 1963–64, the Lakers were 42–38, third in division play. West averaged almost 29 and Baylor 25 points a game, but the St. Louis Hawks eliminated them this time, three games to two in the first round.

In 1964–65, Los Angeles regained first place in the NBA's Western Division. Fred Schaus's team again featured West, second in the NBA at 31 points per game, and Baylor. The West-Baylor duo became the first in league history to score 2,000 points each in a single season. In the playoffs, West scored more than 40 points a game, including a 46.3 per game mark in six games versus Baltimore. However, the lack of a big man was their Achilles' heel. It was the era of the dominant center. In Philadelphia, Wilt Chamberlain defied description. In Boston, Bill Russell controlled the boards. In Los Angeles, Darrall Imhoff was a pale imitation, literally and figuratively.

Imhoff, a seven-footer from the L.A. suburb of Alhambra, had led California to the 1959 national championship, but he never materialized as a great pro. He didn't provide the scoring, rebounding, or defense to compete with the likes of Chamberlain or Russell. With West and Baylor delivering the points, Imhoff was not needed as a scorer, but he had to pound the boards and spearhead the defense. Absent that, West and Baylor found themselves forced to score and score and score in order to keep the Lakers in the game. This was an exhausting formula—one that was destined to fail in the playoffs, as it did when they lost the 1965 Finals in five games to Russell's Celtics.

Though the Lakers had Wilt Chamberlain and other legendary talent during the 1960s, they were frustrated by Bill Russell and the Boston Celtics for much of the decade.

In 1965, industrialist and media magnate Jack Kent Cooke bought the team from Bob Short for $5 million. He immediately set out to remake the team in his image. It would take a few years, but he would succeed. When the City of Los Angeles failed to meet his new arena demands, he built one privately.

The 1965–66 Lakers led the league with a scoring average of 119.5 points per game, led by West with 31. West made 18 of 18 free throws in a single game against Detroit while setting an NBA record of 840 free throws made in the season. Walt Hazzard, who had led UCLA to the national championship, scored almost 14 points a game, but Baylor had an off year, averaging 16.6.

The 45–35 Lakers advanced to the Finals. By this time, the musty old Boston Garden must have seemed more like a House of Horrors. In seven crazy games Boston prevailed, winning a pins-and-needles final contest by only two points (95–93). For West, it was almost unbearable. An intense man anyway, he was beginning to lose his joy for the game. The pressure, intensity, and disappointment of losing was almost too much for him to bear, but he had a long way to go before ultimate victory would come his way.

Injuries to West (15 games missed) and Baylor provided an acute demonstration as to how important those two stars were to the Lakers when they fell all the way to a 36–45 mark in 1966–67. Schaus concluded his seven-year Lakers career with a creditable 315–245 record (.563). When healthy, West still scored at a 29-points-per-game clip, Baylor at 26.6. While it was an unsuccessful year, a new face did appear, one who was not unfamiliar to Los Angeles basketball aficionados.

Gail Goodrich joined his UCLA teammate Walt Hazzard on the Lakers roster. The 6'1" left-handed sharpshooter scored a little

CELEBRITY CORNER

The Lakers-Knicks rivalry over the years has always had the added attraction of celebrity status. Among the most famous and enthusiastic Knicks celebrity fans have been director Spike Lee and actor-director Woody Allen.

over 12 points a game playing on the same floor (the Sports Arena) where he had first led L.A. Poly High to the city championship, then twice directed the Bruins to national championships in the final years before Pauley was built.

The UCLA-Lakers connection, started by Hazzard and then Goodrich, would continue to grow over the years, collegiate basketball's all-time greatest tradition joining forces, so to speak, with what over time might be considered the pro game's most successful dynasty. But in 1967, the Lakers were a long, *long* way from even thinking about having bragging rights over the vaunted Celtics.

That said, an even more disturbing development was afoot in the National Basketball Association that season, at least from L.A.'s standpoint. For years, the Lakers battled Boston, always coming out on the losing end. *If only Boston would falter*, or so the thinking went in some circles, *then Los Angeles could ascend to the top.*

In 1967, Boston did not falter so much as the Philadelphia 76ers announced their presence with the authority of the German army in Poland, 1939. Wilt Chamberlain, Billy Cunningham, and Hal Greer—star players, healthy and in the prime of their careers—formed the nucleus of a team that got hot and stayed hot all season. Philly went 68–13 and then smashed through all playoff opposition to end the Boston run that L.A. had failed to end for years.

By season's end, the below-.500 Lakers were forced to reevaluate their position in the league. If the Sixers were to hold their lofty perch for the next several years, then the bar was extended even higher. They had never reached the lower bar. Changes needed to be made.

When Elgin Baylor injured his knee, it looked like the Lakers' hopes went down the drain. His career appeared to be over, but he said, "The more I thought about it, the more determined" he became to come back and play. West said it was "difficult to accept" watching the great Baylor hobbling about, and that while he did recover and played to a high standard, "he wasn't the Elgin Baylor of old."

Baylor's injury probably cost the Lakers at least two NBA championships. The prospect of Baylor, Chamberlain, and West—all in great health and at the prime of their careers—playing together as a single unit of mind, body, and spirit, conjures the image of all-time greatness. The Lakers of the late 1960s and early 1970s could have been the greatest dynasty ever assembled—a basketball version of Babe Ruth's Yankees or Vince Lombardi's Packers.

Baylor was a game-changing player. Along with Oscar Robertson he helped turn basketball into an athletic, contact sport—a contest of physicality, quickness, and speed. Baylor was the kind of player who did not merely pull up and shoot. He drove, picked up fouls, and created three-point plays.

"It was very, very difficult," he said of his injury. "I would try to do a lot of things that I just couldn't do. It was frustrating."

But Baylor also said that the injury focused him. While his days driving the lane were reduced, he relied on perimeter shooting and posting up. In 1965–66 he reduced his scoring average to 17, but West picked up the slack.

In the first game of the 1966 Finals, Baylor and West led Los Angeles from an 18-point deficit to a 133–129 overtime win, but the Celtics always knew how to capture the psychological battle. After a game in which Baylor scored 36 and West 41, Boston coach Red Auerbach announced he was stepping down as head coach and that his replacement would be Bill Russell. It was a shocking headline—the first African American head coach of a major professional sports franchise, and a player-coach at that. It took all the thunder away from Los Angeles.

John Havlicek took control for the Celtics, who vaulted out to a 3–1 series lead, but then Gail Goodrich was assigned to him and West moved to forward. L.A. struggled back to tie the series at three.

The scene at Boston Garden for Game 7 was utterly chaotic. West and Baylor could not hit the broad side of a barn, but L.A. battled back amid the mayhem, cutting the Celtic lead to six with 20 seconds remaining. Then Massachusetts governor John Volpe decided it was time for Auerbach, in his final game, to light his famed "victory cigar." The fans, seeing the cigar lit, began to rush the floor. Meanwhile, Los Angeles scored to cut the lead to 95–93 with four seconds left.

Amid fans, orange juice containers, people stealing players' shirts, and bedlam, Havlicek dribbled out the clock and it was over.

"We came awfully close to putting that damn thing out," Schaus said of Auerbach's cigar.

Two years later, Schaus retired and the team moved into the Forum. Bill "Butch" van Breda Kolff, known as "the Dutchman," replaced him. Van Breda Kolff had coached Bill Bradley at Princeton and, in keeping with his Ivy League pedigree, impressed Cooke with his articulation. He brought a collegiate style to the team: conditioning, multiple-passing offensive schemes, and bed checks. On the pro level "it didn't work," said West.

Once the Lakers moved into the Forum, they became a new basketball team, rolling to a 30–8 record to close out the 1967–68 season with a 52–30 record.

"That second half of the season, the team realized van Breda Kolff's vision," longtime Lakers scout Bill Bertka said.

Van Breda Kolff found a way to use Imhoff's talent. He realized the big center could not score and dominate as he had at the collegiate level, so he stopped trying to get that out of him. With Baylor recovering and West in his prime, he had plenty of offense. Gail Goodrich drove lanes and could shoot, too, so Imhoff set picks for his teammates.

The Chicago Bulls and the San Francisco Warriors (having lost hotshot scorer Rick Barry to the ABA) were swept aside, but Los Angeles had to sit and wait for Philadelphia and Boston to complete their series. The defending champion 76ers were out to

SOCIAL PROGRESS

"Born 50 or 100 years earlier, most of the tall, strong, fast athletes of today would not be million-dollar superstars but attractions at freak shows."
—Wilt Chamberlain, 1991

assert themselves as the new dominant force in the league. The rivalry between Chamberlain and Russell was at its highest point, with Russell now coaching the Celtics and desperately struggling to maintain the standards set by Auerbach. Much rode on Russell's shoulders. He had his doubters. They came in all colors and from all regions.

Some were in the "Chamberlain camp." Were the Sixers better than the Celtics? Were the Celtics over the hill? What about the Lakers? Were they better than both of the eastern teams?

The Lakers wanted Boston, for three reasons. Chamberlain was so intimidating that they figured he would be harder to contain. If the Celtics were over the hill, they would be an easier opponent. But the biggest reason was that West, Baylor, and their teammates figured they owed something to Boston, like a big fat Finals victory celebration, preferably on their new floor.

Boston crawled back to beat Philly in seven games, helping to cement Russell's place in history and cast doubt on Wilt's. The Lakers were rested and felt they matched up well. Notre Dame's Tommy Hawkins had joined the team and provided depth at the forward position. Boston surely would be emotionally drained and physically beaten down by the seven-game struggle with Chamberlain.

But it did not work out that way. Boston served notice that they were ready, willing, and able to handle L.A. when they held West and Baylor to a combined 18-of-55 shooting in a Game 1 win on the parquet floor of Boston Garden. The Lakers then earned a split going back west.

Boston won at the Forum, but West scored 38, Baylor 30, to even it at two apiece with a 119–105 win. Game 5 in Boston was one for the ages. West, playing on a severely sprained ankle that at first looked bad enough to keep him out, played and starred anyway with 35 points. He led L.A. to a grind-it-out comeback, making a key late steal and pass to a streaking, scoring Baylor. Then after another turnover he scored to tie the game. But Boston persevered on the strength of Russell's shot-blocking and Don Nelson's free throw shooting to win in overtime, 120–117, and take the series lead.

Back in Los Angeles, Russell outcoached van Breda Kolff by moving Sam Jones to forward, where he dominated Goodrich and forced the Lakers into a taller, slower lineup. The blowout victory in front of Cooke and the home fans on the new Forum floor was an indication that despite the new surroundings, it was the same old story.

TAKE A BITE OUT OF THE BIG APPLE

When things go wrong, the coach gets fired. This makes sense in a bottom-line kind of way. The owner will not fire himself. After all, he owns the whole thing.

The general manager will not fire himself. Human nature dictates this.

It is easier to fire one coach than all the players.

Thus, two weeks after the 1969 debacle against Boston, Butch van Breda Kolff resigned to become head coach of the Detroit Pistons. It was a face-saving gesture. Nobody leaves a championship-level team in Los Angeles to take over an also-ran in Detroit.

His replacement was brought in specifically to mollify Wilt Chamberlain. Joe Mullaney announced, "Wilt is special and must be treated special."

Chamberlain liked the idea that his new coach did not want to be his boss, as if the idea that a coach running the show was unheard of. It was players like Chamberlain who made coaches like Bobby Knight decide that the NBA was not for them.

But early in the season an event occurred that changed the entire dynamic of Chamberlain's role with the Lakers. At age 33, having missed only one game per season for his first 11 years, the "indestructible" Chamberlain injured his knee. Doctors told him he was out for the season.

Chamberlain's injury had a silver lining, however. Baylor had stopped driving the lanes and, more important, stopped being a vocal team leader because he was in Wilt's shadow, a sad occurrence in the eyes of teammates and writers who covered the team. With the big man on crutches, Baylor revived his career.

Los Angeles struggled but maintained their position as the "best in the West." But in the East, the New York Knickerbockers surprised everybody by putting together a dream season. In Milwaukee, the expansion Bucks were suddenly a powerhouse led by their awesome rookie, UCLA's Lew Alcindor.

It looked to be an egalitarian landscape come postseason. Boston was out of it, with only John Havlicek left trying to hang on to the old glory. As the playoffs approached, Chamberlain announced his intention to return to the club. The injury was something new for him, but he responded like a champion. He belied his old reputation as a malingerer, lazy, a late riser. Instead, he took to his rehabilitation with a vengeance, determined to come back.

"There's been so much unhappiness connected to my basketball—disappointing defeats, unfair criticism, and such—that I really hadn't realized how much the game meant to me," he said. "I've been surprised at the nice fan mail I've gotten since I've been hurt. I guess getting hurt has made me seem human and has made people sympathize with me for the first time. Usually, I've been regarded as some kind of animal."

It was a telling comment for Wilt at a pivotal point in his career. The period between 1968 and 1970 was one of changing attitudes. The assassinations of Martin Luther King Jr. (Memphis in April 1968) and Bobby Kennedy (at L.A.'s Ambassador Hotel in June 1968), combined with the ongoing Vietnam War and the civil rights movement, all played against a Technicolor, televised, free-love backdrop. Attitudes were changing.

When Chamberlain made his return in time for the playoffs, he was welcomed back by his teammates and the fans. Los Angeles, with a 46–36 record, was immediately installed as either a "wild card" or a favorite to go all the way. If they could reach the Finals, the lack of Russell with those green-clad jerseys and that stinking old Boston Garden, it was like the balm of Gilead. If only...

West scored 31 points a game. He and Baylor both scored over 40 in a single game against the San Francisco Warriors, a feat accomplished by only eight teammates in history. Baylor averaged 24, and Happy Hairston came on to add some punch.

NUMBERS DON'T LIE (OR DO THEY?)

Entering the 2006–07 season, the Lakers were 382–254 (.601), the best playoff record in NBA history. The Knicks were 179–175 (.506).

Everybody was rooting for a New York–Los Angeles Finals. When the Knicks and Lakers both held to form, that is what happened. The Knicks, a perennial loser, electrified the Big Apple with 60 wins under coach Red Holzman, MVP center Willis Reed, guard Walt "Clyde" Frazier, and forwards "Dollar Bill" Bradley and Dave DeBusschere.

At Madison Square Garden, New York ran away with the first game, 124–112. Reed scored 37, mostly from outside. Chamberlain was asked why he did not follow Reed to the perimeter, and he seemed surprised at the prospect before stating, "Next time I will."

Reed was now just a younger, prime-of-his-career version of Russell. A big, strong rebounder and scorer, for the very first time he represented an intimidating force against Wilt Chamberlain. The tables had turned, and it was that old sinking feeling for L.A. The home-court advantage was New York's. The wild crowd made it obvious that if it came to a seventh contest in this building, they would be the Knicks' "sixth man."

This was a new era in New York sports, and in fan participation. For years, the Yankees had dominated New York. They were a corporate team with Wall Street fans, pinstriped fat cats who puffed cigars from expensive box seats. The Yankees had fallen precipitously, however, with the Apple's attentions being directed toward a "new breed" of player and team.

There was "Broadway Joe and the Super Jets," who upset Baltimore in the 1969 Super Bowl. Perhaps for the first time, female fans made their presence wildly known, shrieking and howling over the long-haired sex symbol quarterback, Joe Willie Namath.

They were followed by Tom Seaver and the "Amazin' Mets," an unlikely group of upstarts who energized Shea Stadium crowds

HALL OF THE VERY GOOD

Rudy LaRusso averaged 14.2 points a game for the Lakers between 1960 and 1967.

like nothing anybody had ever heard or seen before en route to winning the 1969 World Series. Each time they clinched—the division title, the National League pennant, the world championship—fans stormed the field en masse. It was utterly unheard of, but the enthusiasm of the Jets and Mets carried right over to the 1969–70 basketball season, which of course came right on the heels of Mets glory.

Madison Square Garden fans, who no longer resembled the suit-and-tie crowd but now had the mod look of a new generation—sideburns, long hair, colorful shirts—adopted this team, implored them to play *"DE-fense,"* and turned the old arena into a nightly party.

New York, a city in cultural, financial, and criminal trouble at this point in time, can trace its eventual comeback in part to the energies of the Jets, Mets, and Knicks. To a player like Jerry West, it was very ominous. He was attuned to all the signs that the stars just might not be aligned in his team's favor. If ever victory was theirs for the taking, it had been a year earlier against the aging Celtics, but now...

All bets were off. Still, Mr. Clutch was bound and determined to be a modern Sir Lancelot, even if the myth of Camelot does end in tragedy. Chamberlain came to play in the second game, when he forced Reed into 17 missed shots and then blocked the Knicks center at the buzzer to preserve a must-win 105–103 victory.

The Finals moved to Los Angeles for the next two games. Game 3 epitomized West's career. On the one hand, he was superhuman, putting on one of the top clutch performances not just in Lakers or basketball history, but in the annals of American sports. On the other hand, he walked away in bitter defeat. It fulfilled his destiny of being the greatest tragic hero the game has ever seen.

It initially looked like the Lakers' night, with West and Baylor burying New York. Chamberlain ruled inside. Forced to the perimeter, New York adjusted and rallied to take the lead in the fourth quarter. Chamberlain tied the game with a free throw with 13 seconds remaining. DeBusschere then pumped one in for a 102–100 Knicks lead.

With three seconds left, Chamberlain figured it was over and made a lazy in-bounds pass to West. But Frazier caught the look in Jerry's eyes, describing him as "crazy," as in, "this guy thinks he's gonna make this" crazy, which he was.

Reed tried to shadow West, who dribbled three times, figured he had a second before the buzzer, and let fly a perfect set shot from 63 yards out. It was farther out than a lot of field goals in football, flew farther than a lot of fly balls in baseball, and swished through the net while DeBusschere threw his hands up in despair before collapsing to the ground.

If it had been Michael Jordan, who seemed to have played under a lucky star his whole career, it would have won the game and spurred his team to the NBA title. Jordan played with the three-point shot. West did not.

Lakers physician Dr. Robert Kerlan jumped up and ran onto the floor, apparently forgetting that he had arthritis (which he had a cane for, but that fell to the ground) and that the two-pointer only tied it instead of winning it. He later told Scott Ostler of the L.A. Times that he felt like a "perfect ass." Chamberlain ran to the locker room, confused about the score and thinking victory was theirs. He returned in time to lose, 111–108.

Baylor dominated Game 4 with 30 points, and the 121–115 overtime win tied the series, but it was clear what was happening. The two teams were trading "field position," but with New York holding the home-court advantage in the form of Game 7 at Madison Square Garden, they had the "hammer."

Form did not play itself out easily, however. Another "let it get away" debacle for Jerry West and his teammates to agonize over occurred in Game 5 at New York. Wilt came on strong and Los Angeles led by 10 points. Then Reed tore a muscle in his thigh and was out, probably for the series.

Finally a break, something going against the other team, and after all L.A. had gone through they would take it and send Willis a get-well card after it was over and won. Chamberlain & Co. took the crowd out of it and increased the lead to 13 at the half.

Bill Bradley—Rhodes scholar, future U.S. senator, and presidential candidate—had an idea. It did not solve the problems of the Middle East, but it did force Wilt to come out from under the basket on defense, which meant New York could get offensive rebounds and find open men down low. Bradley's suggestion was a 3–2 zone offense, something from the archaic college game.

"Outside we had two wings with a point man," Bradley explained. "Inside we had one guy on the baseline and a roamer. When we saw Wilt playing a man, it was like attacking a zone. Just hit the open spaces in a zone."

The 1969–70 Knickerbockers had talent, but their greatest attributes were heart, guts, and smarts. They adapted to Bradley's suggestion and made it succeed. On offense, Los Angeles began to panic. Without Reed defending them, they had mismatches in their favor but started to press, with the Knicks whittling the score down to a manageable seven-point deficit entering the final quarter. But the key was the crowd: 19,500 fans cheering, "Let's go, Knicks." New York fans had unnerved the Raiders, the Colts, the Cubs, the Braves, the Orioles; now they were unnerving the Lakers.

When Bradley's jumper tied the score at 87 with just under eight minutes left, it was identical to the previous September, when the Mets beat the Cubs at Shea Stadium, forcing a tie in the National League East. Technically, the two teams had the same chance of winning, but the momentum had swung so far in favor of the Mets, coming from nine and a half out in about a month, that the season was over. The Los Angeles Lakers were as beaten as Leo Durocher's Cubs had been, and it showed as the Knicks cruised to the 107–100 victory.

DeBusschere called it "one of the greatest games ever played." West and Chamberlain walked forlornly off the court. Jerry had no second-half field goals, Wilt just four points.

DE-fense.

TAKE THIS GAME...

Tommy Hawkins came out of Notre Dame and played five seasons for the Lakers. He became a popular broadcaster in Los Angeles, worked for the Dodgers, and now cohosts a luncheon with USC's Craig Fertig every even year called "The Game Is On," held the week of the USC–Notre Dame football contest at the Coliseum.

So L.A. came home and rolled over, playing dead before the home folks in a Game 6 loss that gave New York its first NBA title, right? Hey, this is the Lakers, and don't forget it. In Game 6 they defeated the Knicks so thoroughly and so completely as to totally swing the momentum their way, leading most pundits to actually believe they would win the seventh game.

The Knicks had no Reed. They were physically and mentally exhausted, drained, done. Chamberlain's 45-point effort was reminiscent of his salad days in Philadelphia. He killed the boards, and his team toyed with New York like adults playing with children, except they did not toy with them. They beat them to a pulp, 135–113.

Then Wilt opened his big mouth. He told the press that his team had done a fantastic job just to get where they were, complaining about the nature of American sports fans who, according to the film *Patton,* which was playing to packed theaters that very night, "Will not tolerate a loser, because the very thought of losing is hateful...to Americans."

Wilt seemed positively French in his appraisal of things, lamenting that the fans could not simply "enjoy great games between great teams." West just shook his head. He was most definitely American and could describe with acute accuracy just what it felt like to play at the highest level imaginable—only to lose—and in this regard Jerry was unquestionably of the *"Patton* school." To him, losing was what losing meant to soldiers. You did not just shake hands and go home; you were probably dead or in a POW camp. He felt like a prisoner and would not free himself until victory was secure.

What happened next goes down in history with Babe Ruth's "called shot"...Joe DiMaggio emerging from the disabled list to lead the Yanks to four straight at Fenway in 1949...Johnny Lujack tackling Doc Blanchard to save the game for the Irish against Army in 1946. The stuff of lore, of legend, of courage.

Bradley and DeBusschere approached Reed and asked him to give them 20 minutes. Just his presence in uniform would be enough. Don't wear street clothes, they begged him. Reed said he would take injections and hope for the best. No promises.

The teams warmed up. Knicks fans filed into Madison Square Garden, and their hearts sank when they did not spot Willis Reed. On TV and the radio, announcers lamented to the populace that it looked as if their MVP center was not going to make it. Bradley's homemade "3–2 zone" was not going to work. They could not hold Goliath back any longer. Wilt's 45 points and 27 rebounds in Game 6 hovered over them like Nazi soldiers in the streets of 1940 Paris.

In the locker room, the Knicks medical staff approached Reed. He needed injections of carbocaine and cortisone if he hoped to even walk, much less run up and down the floor. The needle was produced. Like a scene in the movies, liquid dripped off the tip, Willis's horrified expression in the background. Here was the problem. Willis Reed was a big man, and the biggest part of his body was his thighs. *Thunder thighs*, they called them. It was what made him so strong, such a great rebounder, so difficult to move in the paint, but in order for the medicine to reach the injury, which was a deep tear, that needle needed to drill like an oil rig in the Texas panhandle.

The needle was huge, and the doctor made contact with Reed's skin, then kept plowing and plowing until his fist was

IN THE BEGINNING

Walt Hazzard, the Lakers' first pick in the 1964 draft out of UCLA, is an alum of Wilt Chamberlain's school, Overbrook High in Philadelphia.

touching the thigh. Reed almost passed out. Still, the doctor had to move it around to make sure the carbocaine and cortisone got to the precise location of the injury, which of course meant the needle was probing and stinging an already-torn muscle that hurt like the dickens without the needle.

Reed just thought about a championship ring. Maybe he found religion. However he got through the experience, he did not faint. He got wrapped up, strapped on his shoes, and emerged from the locker room. His teammates, who up until then did not know if he would play, saw the big man hobbling out toward them. It was like Sandy Koufax, who used to say that the pain from the treatments was worse than the pain of pitching. After the needle, playing basketball was child's play.

The Lakers saw the same thing and responded like Apollo Creed when he sees that Rocky has not stayed on the canvas.

The fans? Those who were at Madison Square Garden on May 8, 1970, say the response was unlike anything else they ever heard in their lives. One of them was William Goldman, an Academy Award–winning screenwriter who loved the Knicks so much he missed the ceremony in Hollywood to see the Knicks play in New York. He later said the scene was more dramatic than anything he ever wrote in *Butch Cassidy and the Sundance Kid*, *Marathon Man*, or any of his other thrillers.

"The scene is indelibly etched in my mind," Walt Frazier recalled, "because if that did not happen, I know we would not have won the game."

Awash in emotion, the game started up. At tip-off, Reed told Chamberlain, "I can't go to my right all that well." Wilt just stared at him. Reed could never go to his right anyway.

Reed looked immobile until the game started. He got the ball and made the Knicks' first two shots, eliciting chaos. Somehow, he jammed up against Chamberlain, and oddly the injury played to his favor in a way. Harassed by Reed, Wilt was unsure how to deal with his opponent and made only two of his first nine shots. Emotion usually lasts only a short while. On this night it was an active component in New York's favor from tip to buzzer. They led early and by larger and larger margins. Reed was of little consequence offensively after the first shots, but his presence was magical. He left the game to a standing ovation that elevated him into the Big Apple pantheon with Ruth, Mantle, Gifford—61–37 Knicks at the time, 113–99 final.

Writers described the Los Angeles dressing room as a "morgue." Wilt was given the opportunity to blame his knee injury, but he accepted his responsibility in the loss like a man.

The defeats to Boston, even the previous year's Game 7 shocker at home, it all had added up, and now the team seemed to have been lost to a deep depression that would last another year. In 1970–71 the Lakers went through the motions. The league realigned divisions, and Milwaukee, now in the West featuring Lew Alcindor and Oscar Robertson, swept them aside four games to one. Mullaney was fired. They were old, disconsolate. There was little reason to believe happy days were ahead.

DADDY DEAREST

THE ROYAL CANADIAN

Jack Kent Cooke—who, like so many who succeeded in Los Angeles, was not originally from there—symbolized L.A. in the 1960s. The old ways were out. The new ways were in. The new ways were ways of excellence, productivity, and creativity. The Lakers were a haphazard operation under Bob Short, but they became an efficient operation under the perfectionist Cooke.

He was brusque. He wrote memos. He was detail oriented. He noticed everything and expected it to be corrected, pronto. He shouted. He was like George Steinbrenner before Steinbrenner, a new kind of owner at a time when owners were rich old guys who bought teams so they could invite their drinking buddies to watch games with them.

"He was the number one asshole who ever lived," said "Hot Rod" Hundley, who was a Lakers broadcaster under Cooke. "He was totally, absolutely, unbelievably wrapped up in himself and had no respect for anyone but himself."

"Everybody was on eggshells," recalled John Radcliffe, a Lakers statistician. "We were afraid to make a mistake, because we were gonna get yelled at. It was his style. He didn't hold anything back."

"Mr. Cooke shouted and screamed at anyone who didn't give him perfection," said scout Bill Bertka. "He was interested in the bottom line, in success, in winning. That's all he wanted."

The self-made Jack Kent Cooke relentlessly bent the franchise to his will and pointed the Lakers in the right direction after becoming owner of the team in the 1960s.

Cooke once invited Bertka to his home for a breakfast meeting and asked him if he wanted a cup of coffee, to which Bertka replied, "That would be nice." Cooke responded that he didn't care whether it was nice or not. "Do you want a cup of coffee?"

Bertka said that Cooke's goal was to put people on "the defensive." Legendary basketball guru Pete Newell—who coached California to the 1959 national championship, helped build the Lakers dynasty, modernize basketball, and restructure the dynamics of center play in the NBA (his "Big Man Campuses" became a model for development of post players)—took to Cooke's style. The owner insisted on recording every phone call, a tool Newell found valuable to him when talking trade or contract with fellow executives or agents.

Like A's owner Charlie O. Finley, Cooke required his employees to be "on call 24 hours a day, because Jack was on call 24 hours a day," said Newell.

In an age before cell phones, Cooke demanded that his key people be near a phone and stay in contact so they could be reached at hotels, restaurants, dinner parties, and the like. He wanted discipline and punctuality. Still, Cooke understood the "big issues," according to Newell, letting an "honest $50,000 mistake go by without comment," then yelling over "pocket change."

Cooke was not the type to get flustered, and this attitude carried over to his employees, much the way a calm general or president exudes control in a time of crisis. At first, Cooke's greatest contribution came in the form of marketing and promotions. But he was so hands-on he couldn't help but learn the inner game of basketball.

Few owners have ever succeeded at this, no matter how hard they try. The only exception seems to be Finley, who, despite having played only some American Legion ball, was either a baseball genius or the luckiest man in the world when every move he made fell into place during his building of the three-time world champion Oakland A's.

Cooke studied and listened. His ego got the best of him. He came to the conclusion that he knew basketball the way a Pete Newell, a Tex Winter, a Jerry West knows basketball.

"He didn't know," said West.

Cooke hailed from Canada. He was a self-made man, a natural salesman who by dint of hard work succeeded in the capitalist shark tank. He made his mark in the radio business and moved, like so many others with a dream but no pedigree, to California. Once he made his money, he tried to reinvent himself as an "old money" figure, effectuating the three-name affectation. He no doubt would have loved to be *Sir* or *Lord* Jack Kent Cooke, as his benefactor, Lord Thomson, a British media magnate, was known.

Cooke's uniform design, the choice of purple that he called "Forum blue," and his vision of a stadium modeled after the Acropolis gave the scent of a man who thought of himself as vaguely European and indeed aristocratic.

He saw sports as the leisure activity of a king, so to speak, and went after the Angels franchise that Finley and Short wanted. Gene Autry landed it. Denied a spot in baseball, he set his sights on basketball and ice hockey, the latter a natural for a Canadian but alien to the Southern California landscape.

It was his pursuit of a hockey franchise that led him to the building of the Forum. In 1965, the Sports Arena was only six years old and perfectly acceptable for basketball. But a minor league hockey team played at the Sports Arena, and the city rebuffed Cooke's attempts to secure an NHL franchise for the building. He then went out and built the Forum for the Kings *and* the Lakers.

When Jack Kent Cooke opened his "Fabulous Forum" during the 1967–68 season, he became a symbol of can-do L.A., the city of the future, where private enterprise could solve the woes of society. The Lakers were the "new breed," ushering an old league into modern times. His team, like actresses in nearby Hollywood, underwent a facelift in their first season. Throughout the year it looked like it was a winning formula. Bill van Breda Kolff took over as the coach. The team changed their color scheme, in accordance with Cooke's love of the color purple. The reason he called it "Forum blue" was because he loved the color, not the word. It would be the Lakers' uniform style until the Shaq O'Neal–Kobe Bryant era.

THEN CAME SHARMAN

He did not arrive on a white horse. He was a great athlete, but not ballyhooed as a great coach. His old-school style was immediately berated as "yesterday." He would not be able to relate to the modern athlete, and in particular he and Wilt Chamberlain would blend like oil and water.

In truth, however, Bill Sharman was the Lakers' savior, the man who brought them deliverance. But he was not Jack Kent Cooke's first choice. The obvious guy, if he could get him, was right there in his backyard, or more accurately down the road, literally, from Cooke's Bel Air mansion. John Wooden was at the

California native Bill Sharman provided the strong personalities on the early 1970s Lakers with no-nonsense coaching and helped forge a championship team. Photo courtesy of Bettmann/CORBIS.

height of his powers at UCLA. He was presiding over the greatest dynasty in the history of big-time collegiate sports. In 1971, the Bruins had just won their fifth-straight NCAA basketball championship—their seventh in eight years.

Wooden's reputation was utterly flawless; he was called "St. John" because he did not swear, drink, or chase women. He was Christian, moral..."perfect." In the end, it was these qualities that probably made him *imperfect* for the job of Lakers coach, but the idea of Wooden moving from Westwood to Inglewood was tantalizing...to Lakers and Trojans fans, at least.

Cooke saw in him the kind of coach who related to African Americans, who made up the core of his team (Chamberlain, of course, and at the time Baylor, before injury forced his retirement). Cooke invited St. John to his home for tea in the library.

NICKNAMES

Elgin Baylor was called "Motormouth" because he talked so much. He nick-named Jerry West "Zeke from Cabin Creek," because West grew up near Cabin Creek, West Virginia. Jerry was kidded about his background a lot. Some people called him "Beverly Hillbilly" after the popular TV show of that era.

After discussing religion, poetry, art, and history, the question was raised: would the man they called "Coach" be willing to take a pay hike from his UCLA salary, then in the $25,000 to $30,000 range, to an offer of over $100,000, which is what it was assumed Cooke was willing to part with?

"I've had my time," Wooden told Cooke. "I'm too old to start in professional basketball."

There have been two schools of thought regarding this state of affairs. Wooden himself has shown some disdain for the pro game: its lack of defensive intensity; the greedy, money-hungry players; lack of discipline; the superstar syndrome that elevates player over coach. On the other hand, he was a consummate pro-fessional. Everybody respected him. He knew the game back and forth. His manner was so gentle that even players like Wilt Chamberlain would have been in awe of him, seeing him as just the guy to lead a team of lost souls to the Promised Land.

But Wooden's answer was final. He returned to UCLA and his greatest teams—Bill Walton's 1972 and 1973 national champions; an 88-game winning streak; his 10th NCAA title in 12 seasons; a salary that topped out at $35,000; and then, in 1975, retirement to a life of grandchildren and reverence.

But Jack Kent Cooke had a Wooden *type* in mind. Bill Sharman was not Wooden...or was he? In a number of ways, he was a clone of John Wooden. He was everything Wooden was except for seven national championships, but the rest of his résumé was stellar, with remarkable similarities to the Wizard of Westwood.

Sharman grew up in middle-class surroundings in Porterville, a town located between Fresno and Yosemite in central California, but moved to Los Angeles, where he starred at Narbonne High School near San Pedro. He served in the navy and played basketball and baseball at USC, leading the Trojans to victories over Wooden's Bruins. He was part of a golden age of basketball at Troy in the wake of Sam Barry's introduction of the triangle offense.

Basketball was his sport, but so was baseball. He rode the Brooklyn Dodgers' pine down the stretch of the ill-fated 1951 pennant loss to the Giants. The NBA was forming into a well-respected league. He went with the Boston Celtics, becoming one of their all-time greats. He earned four rings in an 11-year career and was considered the greatest shooter of his era, as well as one of the finest free throw artists ever. Sharman was in such great physical condition that he ran rings around his opponents. His shooting technique was honed to such a degree that he was as sure from the floor as any player ever.

Upon retirement Sharman got into coaching. He won a championship in the old ABL; was offered the job as USC coach by athletic director Jess Hill, but turned it down; and in 1971 led the Utah Stars to the American Basketball Association championship.

His similarities to Wooden included the fact that he was a great player. He was a baseball star, a sport Wooden always said was his favorite. He was old school, a gentleman, happily married, honorable. He had the imprimatur of a winner, draped in Celtic glory, and winning an ABA title did not hurt. Being a Los Angeleno and a Trojan were considered pluses, too.

Fred Schaus liked Sharman, whom he recognized as a college type who had transitioned to the pro game as a player and coach. Sharman had earlier turned a bad Cal State–Los Angeles team into winners, and in 1967 his San Francisco Warriors made it to the Finals before succumbing to Chamberlain's 76ers. Schaus, whose advice was respected by Cooke, recommended the 45-year-old Sharman.

In later years Cooke recalled an "inner intensity" in Sharman that reminded him of Joe Gibbs, who would coach the Cooke-owned Washington Redskins to three Super Bowl championships. Sharman, however, was getting a lot of negativity from his personal circle, the argument being that Los Angeles was old and that a first-year NBA coach should start with a team on the way up, not vice versa. Much of that, however, came from the Celtic crowd, who found it incongruous that one of their own would attach himself to *those people!*

For Sharman, it was an easy decision, however. First, the chance to be a head coach in the National Basketball Association again was an opportunity that he could not pass up. Despite his Boston pedigree, he was still a Southern Californian. Cooke paid well, the Lakers were a first-class outfit, and he could live with his wife near the beach. Finally, there was the chance to coach Baylor, West, and Chamberlain. The Chamberlain case was seen as an obstacle, but Sharman knew that coaches must have great players, and these were superstars. Any great coach must have confidence and—no matter how politely it is manifested—a big ego. Sharman's ego told him that he could motivate Wilt Chamberlain.

He did not yet know that Baylor was nine games away from retirement. But West was any coach's dream.

"Egads, they were prima donnas," Cooke recalled of the 1971–72 Lakers.

And there were new personalities in the dressing room, all fitting in with the new sensibilities of Los Angeles in the early 1970s. Happy Hairston was called a "locker-room lawyer" by Lakers historian Roland Lazenby. Jim McMillian was an Ivy Leaguer. Gail Goodrich was back from exile in Phoenix, and he was a winner with UCLA ties.

It was a golden age in L.A. and in the state of California in terms of sports, culture, and politics. Aside from the Lakers, UCLA was in the middle of their unparalleled basketball run. Across town, Southern California's 1972 football team is still considered the greatest of all time. The Trojans won almost every year in track and baseball, too.

Up the coast, the Oakland A's were about to win the first of their three straight world championships. The Oakland Raiders were one of the most exciting teams ever assembled. At a time when attendance was down in other cities, Los Angeles was thought of as the "sports capital of the world." They had the best

TRADING PLACES

Jack Kent Cooke was the driving force behind the trade that involved the Lakers sending their two first-round draft picks, Dave Meyers and Junior Bridgeman, plus Elmore Smith and Brian Winters, to the Bucks for Kareem Abdul-Jabbar in 1975.

stadiums, drew the biggest crowds, had the best teams, and were awash in glamour. L.A. replaced New York as the "in" city of the United States.

Politically, California's Richard Nixon won 62 percent of the vote and 49 of 50 states in capturing the 1972 presidential election. His "shadow," Ronald Reagan, was in his second successful term as governor of California, on his way to the White House and the immortality that Nixon squandered away.

It was a boom time for the economy of the state and the city: expansion, growth, freeways, high-rises, and a shift in financial power from old Eastern money to California's real estate, technology, and aerospace sectors. In Hollywood, it had never been better: *The Godfather, Patton,* and *The French Connection.*

The beautiful people of Tinseltown (a notoriously fickle lot who shifted their passions from the Trojans to the Bruins to the Dodgers to the Angels to the Rams to the Raiders to the Kings to the Mighty Ducks...) in 1971–72 found themselves beating a path to the corner of Manchester and Prairie to watch the Wilt and West Show.

Riding the bench: Pat Riley, a Kentuckian by way of New York, embarking on his long-hair-and-beard, check-out-the-chicks-at-Santa-Monica-Beach period; Keith Erickson, an *actual* beach-volleyball type from UCLA; Flynn Robinson, a man of self-concept.

"On that one team you probably had more diverse, strong personalities than you had on any championship team in the history of the game," Bill Bertka said in Roland Lazenby's *The Lakers: A Basketball Journey.*

Sharman had a huge challenge—to mold this disparate group into champions. Few thought it could be done. Wilt was such a veteran by then that he was totally set in his ways, but by the same token he was quite content with himself and his place in the game's history, so there was a sanguine quality that had been missing from his earlier days. Wilt remained confident without being bloodthirsty.

West was soured, like an idealistic politician who had seen too much corruption and bribery. He viewed Sharman as just another guy sent in to reform a system that just might not be reformable, but as the consummate professional he gave all he had until the day he retired. Retirement *was* on his mind, not because his skills were deteriorating, but because the weight of disappointment was almost too much for him to continue to live with. On the other hand, if he were to retire, that would be the end of it. It would be admitting he had failed and would never reach his goals. As long as he strapped it on, there was a chance.

"We had a lot of players who'd had a lot of personal success but hadn't enjoyed team success," West said, in a statement that says everything about him and the American sports ethic. Division championships, great records, Finals appearances—all the earmarks of a great team at the top of the competitive food chain—did not equate "team success" to West. All he had to say about his previous 11 years as a surefire Hall of Famer and L.A. icon was that it was "frustrating" and "terrible."

However, Bill Bertka pointed out that of all the strong personalities, none were stronger than Sharman. In this respect he at least seemed different from John Wooden and therefore better suited to the Los Angeles Lakers than the Bruins coach would have been, although Wooden's quiet demeanor belied great intensity.

Sharman was "on fire," a man at his career peak; the opportunity of a lifetime was laid out before him, and he was determined to make the very most of it. He was a great communicator in the manner of self-motivation guru Tony Robbins, and he lived each waking minute dedicated to productivity. In this respect, Sharman represented the kind of intelligence, drive, and work ethic that, applied to any endeavor—politics, sales, war, sports—had as good a chance at succeeding as possible.

Sharman also had the mark of all great athletes and coaches: "killer instinct."

"Bill matched mine," said Celtics teammate Bob Cousy. In Boston he had gotten into his share of fights, only they were not fights. He did not brawl. He did not "get into it." That was a waste of time. If his ire was up and somebody had to go down, he did it with a minimum of motion. One punch and it was over, as in the case of 6'9", 230-pound Syracuse Nationals Hall of Famer Andy Phillips, who never saw it comin'.

Fighting was semi-encouraged in order to generate fan excitement in the 1950s, not unlike the way it is in hockey today. To Sharman's way of thinking, it was not something he wanted to do, but there were players who felt they could "kind of take advantage of you" unless forced to back off. On the court, Sharman had a driven personality—always thinking, communicating, teaching, demonstrating. Unlike Bill van Breda Kolff and Joe Mullaney, this was a bona fide Hall of Fame player, not that far removed from four world titles, so his word carried genuine respect from the get-go.

Off the court, Sharman was gentle and caring. His relationship with his wife was an extraordinary love affair. He was almost a New Age, Aquarius figure, as comfortable in the funky Venice Beach scene as in Boston Garden. He was balanced, neat, and totally organized. He kept records of opponents, was a stickler for technique, and is thought to be one of the finest—if not *the* finest—fundamental shooters and teachers of the art who ever lived. His preparation was legendary. He was into diet and exercise decades before it became popular, engendering good-natured ribbing over his California ways because he disdained red meat.

On the Celtics he eschewed partying, but with the Lakers he treated his players like adults as long as they were prepared when the bell rang. Sharman was into stretching and conditioning before others were. He was a jogger, a familiar sight on

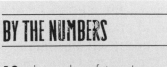

BY THE NUMBERS

13—the number of times Jerry West was selected for the All-Star Game.

the Strand near his Playa del Rey home. He also believed in morning "shootarounds," in which the team would have a light workout and get a feel for the court the day of a game. It was unheard of before he came along, but after his team went 69–13 and took home the brass ring, everybody did it, continuing to this day. He was a visionary and innovator in the world of sports, basketball, and fitness.

He also hired an assistant coach, which at that time was unusual. Today, pro basketball teams have an entourage to rival the Rolling Stones, but back then it was not generally done. Sharman's guy was K.C. Jones. Another Celtic. A Lakers killer. Oh blarney.

Sharman meticulously went about his business, slowly but surely getting the key people to buy into his system. Chick Hearn needed to be convinced. He was considered the Lakers' "assistant." Sharman and Jones planned to institute a Red Auerbach–style fast-break offense, which seemed preposterous considering that Chamberlain was the very essence of the slow-it-down, set-'em-up-low approach.

Sharman, a man of class and respect, invited Chamberlain to lunch at a pricey L.A. eatery. He laid out his approach to Wilt, asking him to give everything he had. Chamberlain saw something in Sharman he had not seen in any coach since Bill's USC teammate Alex Hannum coached the 76ers to the 1967 NBA title. The sale was made, but upon leaving, Sharman, red-faced, announced that he had forgotten his wallet. Wilt picked up the tab with laughter and flourish, as was his style.

Hairston's role was spelled out: rebounding. Cooke rewarded him with a raise and he was grateful. Goodrich was *thrilled* to learn that he would be running the break just like he and Walt Hazzard had done in college. His partner was Jerry West again, which is like asking Johnny Depp if he would like to work with Al Pacino in another movie. West had some knee problems early so Gail had to handle some of the burden, but it was the opportunity that turned him from a good player into a Hall of Famer.

Goodrich was a player's player. His father, Gail Goodrich Sr., had once captained the USC Trojans, and it was assumed the son was ticketed for University Park, too. In his junior year, Goodrich led Poly High to the L.A. city title at the Sports Arena. John Wooden was in the stands. He turned to his assistant, Denny Crum, and announced that the short, unheralded Poly guard could play for him at UCLA.

A man sitting in front of Wooden overheard him, turned around, and asked, "Do you mean that?"

"I certainly do," replied Wooden.

The man sitting in front of Wooden was Gail Goodrich Sr.

Trojan or no Trojan, Goodrich knew that Wooden was the best coach in the country, and he directed his son to Westwood, where All-American honors and national titles waited for him. He had started out in L.A., done time in Phoenix, and now here he was playing for...a Trojan.

Sharman entered a profession in which teams played 82 regular-season games. Therefore, the conventional wisdom held that because of the hardships of travel, schedule, and time constraints, it was impossible to truly prepare for opponents or to place real emphasis on individual contests. "You win some, you lose some," was the motto. A loss was not to be taken too harshly, a victory not particularly celebrated. There was always tomorrow. No single game meant much. Teams had to preserve their energy for the postseason.

But Sharman changed all of that. He became coach of the Lakers just as the money was starting to get really good, and he figured these were well-paid professionals who owed their employers their best efforts every day just as people in any other profession did. He expected them to be students of the game. He was the first coach to truly break down film with his assistants and go over it with the team. Occasional boredom was broken up with spliced footage of soft-core porn to keep them interested.

Sharman approached individual NBA games in the manner of a football coach who has to prepare for only one game per week. His style led to the use of computers and a professional *ethos* in basketball and baseball in which every game is prepared for as if it were Game 7 of the playoffs.

In this regard, Sharman started a mind-set in which much more was expected of professional athletes. It became no longer

HALL OF THE VERY GOOD

Mitch Kupchak was an All-American at North Carolina. He became a vital member of the Lakers in the mid-1980s, and after retirement he became one of the leading executives in the game. He has won five NBA titles as a member of the Lakers' front office, becoming general manager and head of basketball operations.

accepted, even laughed at, for a player to show up hungover, addled by drugs, or forced to pop amphetamines in order to find the motivation to play.

His "shootarounds" were a novelty to the Lakers, who, like most pro athletes, considered the morning to be time reserved for postparty recovery and getting rid of last night's "fiancée." Chamberlain would have laughed at van Breda Kolff or Mullaney had they suggested that Big Norman be at practice before noon, but Wilt had a sense of history combined with a hunger for victory. Bill Sharman had four NBA championship rings, so he was going to give the man the benefit of the doubt. Besides, off the court, Sharman charmed Wilt and everybody else with his redoubtable sunny disposition.

When training camp started, the questions revolved around the 13-year veteran and team captain, Elgin Baylor. It was ironic that Sharman, a fast-break coach of the first order, was introducing an offensive scheme that would have been perfect for Baylor in his prime. Only now the old man, wracked by pain from leg injuries, was immobile.

Enter Jim McMillian. Bill Bertka had scouted him at Columbia and was impressed with the way he handled Villanova's Howard Porter, the 1971 NCAA Tournament's Most Valuable Player. Most basketball people were shocked when Los Angeles made him the 13th pick of the draft. Jack Kent Cooke yelled at Fred Schaus after hearing from sources that it was an ill-advised pick. But Bertka liked McMillian's Ivy League intelligence and work ethic, which under Bill Sharman fit like a glove.

He was short and a bit overweight, but Sharman the health nut was just what the doctor ordered. His grapefruit diet, intense practice sessions, and constant fast-break offense had McMillian in the trim in no time. When Baylor retired, McMillian was the perfect replacement.

When Baylor called it quits, the team was 6–3, but Sharman made it clear he was not satisfied. This was a new concept in pro basketball, where the season tends to play out like a marathon instead of the sprint Sharman foresaw. Sprint is what they did: 33 straight wins. It was truly a thing of beauty, but the pundits questioned Sharman all along. True, he had a great regular-season team, and that was wonderful, but would they have anything left for the "second season," the playoffs, when Big Lew (now Kareem Abdul-Jabbar) and Willis Reed would no doubt be waiting for them?

Replacing Baylor with McMillian—when Sharman told him, Baylor up and retired right then and there—was a melancholy act for Sharman.

"I knew he felt bad, and I wanted him to keep playing," said Sharman. "But he said if he couldn't play up to his standards he would retire."

Cooke described the 33-game winning streak as "one of the happiest times of my life," better even than his Redskins winning Super Bowls. The nature of a winning streak is that it just builds and builds, especially in an "every other day" sport like pro basketball, where anticipation is constantly being rewarded. The 1971–72 Lakers' winning streak occurred while UCLA was building their 88-game college streak (1971–74) over at Pauley. Years later, it was reminisced about when USC ran a 34-game football winning streak starting in 2003 and ending in 2006.

The Lakers' winning streak gives their 1971–72 team a special place in basketball history. While the 1966–67 76ers enjoyed a record almost as good, and the 1995–96 Chicago Bulls broke the Lakers mark, neither ran a winning streak like that.

With Baylor's retirement, Sharman asked West and Chamberlain to assume the role of cocaptains. West, the natural leader of the team, was so humble that he did not feel comfortable with it, but Chamberlain saw it as one of the highlights of his career. For years he had gone his own way, infuriating coaches, teammates, fans, and media with outrageous behavior, and even when he did walk the straight and narrow, it always went crooked.

The fast-break style now fit him perfectly. His scoring records were utterly secure; there was nothing more to be proved. Concentrating on the boards, he pulled down massive rebounding numbers, but unlike the ball-slapping of past years he fired quick outlets to the speedy Goodrich, who must have thought he was back at UCLA, running Michigan ragged in the Final Four.

Goodrich, West, and McMillian, whose weight-loss regimen could be called "run, run, and run some more," were in great shape from training camp, greater shape through Sharman's in-season conditioning regimen, and in even better shape because they were enthused by success. The fast-break action energized them instead of enervating them. On defense Chamberlain became a force like never before, blocking shots, directing them to a teammate in Russell style, and away they went.

Victory number 25 came in Wilt's hometown of Philadelphia, 154–132, with Chamberlain dominating with 32 points, 34 rebounds, and 12 blocks. His scoring records did not approach his halcyon years in Philly, but as an all-around team player, Chamberlain was as thoroughly intimidating as any player ever had been.

On December 22 Los Angeles defeated Baltimore 127–120 for number 27, beating the all-time baseball record of 26 straight by the 1916 New York Giants, and thus setting a new professional standard. Baylor and Philadelphia's Billy Cunningham said that the 35-year-old Chamberlain should win the league's Most Valuable Player award. In 1971–72, Sharman conveyed his considerable knowledge to Chamberlain on the art of free throw shooting. The result was that Wilt became an expert...in practice. He was psyched out during the games and continued to miss.

"I never could figure out how to help him with free throws," Sharman lamented.

The Lakers were big news, their story splashed all over the *Times, Sports Illustrated, Sporting News,* and national television. The NBA loved them. The Forum was jammed every night. It was a phenomenon. But the big story was Chamberlain. Sharman was seen as some kind of Svengali who had turned the troublesome Chamberlain into the ultimate unselfish team player. If *this* Wilt had come out to play in each of the previous 12 years, he would have won more titles than Russell, it was said.

"I don't think I should get the credit," said Sharman. "He's always had a bad rap. Whatever they ask of him he's done. He's just doing more things better now that he is not mainly a scorer. He must block a zillion shots a game. And he scares guys out of other shots or makes them take bad shots."

Chamberlain smiled and opened up to the media. He was articulate and spoke his mind. He expressed amazement that he could score less, and that this somehow allowed his team to score *more*. The Lakers would pass the 100-point mark in 81 of 82 regular-season games, score 162 against the Warriors, and win that one by a record 63 points.

"It's like asking Babe Ruth not to hit home runs, just bunt," he said of his paltry 15-points-per-game scoring average. The entire dynamic of the season was an object lesson in fundamental basketball, where coaches forever told players to sacrifice, to pass the ball; but here was proof positive that the philosophy was not just coachspeak.

As for the shootarounds, Chamberlain reluctantly admitted they were a positive for the team, although he did not personally find improvement in his performance because of them. But the camaraderie of his teammates was worth 81 100-point games.

On January 9, 1972, Los Angeles was 39–3. The warm-weather Lakers entered freezing cold Milwaukee, Wisconsin. Waiting for them: the defending NBA champion Bucks, led by the most dom-

FAMILY TIES

Jeanie Buss, daughter of Jerry Buss, got her start as general manager of the Los Angeles Strings of World Team Tennis.

inant superstar of the new era, the renamed Kareem Abdul-Jabbar. A national television audience tuned in to one of the most bally-hooed regular-season games in pro history.

Bucks coach Larry Costello pulled out all the stops. He scouted L.A. as if it were the playoffs, devising a defense designed to stop the running game. It was an eventful contest. The Bucks halted the L.A. juggernaut, 120–104. It was an ominous sign. Milwaukee had beaten Los Angeles in five games in the 1971 playoffs. They were no longer in the East, having been reassigned in the wake of an expanded league to the Western Conference, where they would have to be handled in a best-four-of-seven series if the Lakers had any hope of even *getting* to the Finals.

It was always something: Russell, Reed, and now Abdul-Jabbar, who from all appearances looked better than any of his predecessors. It was particularly troubling from Chamberlain's angle. Wilt was proud, but here was a 7'2" basketball *wunderkind* who seemed utterly unstoppable. He had done things at UCLA that no collegian had ever thought of doing, carrying that dominance into the league. Abdul-Jabbar at that time was larger than life. Few players loomed so large over his sport. The Lakers were faced with the prospect of being a regular-season champion and a playoff chump. The press played every angle, much of it centered on criticism of Sharman for wearing his guys out in "meaningless" regular-season games, and of Chamberlain, for having the audacity to be a mere human being.

But the end of the winning streak was not all there was to it. Sharman, whose wife was battling health problems at the time, was under stress, too. He yelled at his team in practice and during the games, but in Milwaukee his throat got very sore. He opened his mouth but nothing came out, it got so bad. He went to a doctor in L.A. and was told he had damaged his vocal cords and would have to *shut up for 10 weeks!* He tried a battery-operated megaphone, but it did not work over the crowd noise so he just kept yelling, thinking in the off-season the damage would heal. It never did. It eventually forced him from coaching. To this day he can hardly be heard. He coached the second half of the 1971–72 season with a barely audible rasp.

Los Angeles won 30 of their last 40 games, which is a tremendous record but oddly seemed a letdown after the winning streak. The team's terrible playoff history loomed over them.

"We were waiting for something to happen, something bad to happen," said Riley.

The regular season concluded and another record was theirs: 69–13, one win better than Wilt's 1967 76ers. Everybody started in on whether the '67 Sixers were better than the '72 Lakers, but of course victory would have to be secured in the postseason before Sharman's team could make any claims.

It was a tense period of time. There was no room for error. If *this* team fell, then the franchise was cursed. Nobody even wanted to *think* about what West would do. The writers came up with all kinds of unkind scenarios describing the magnitude of Chamberlain's place in the pantheon of the most overrated athletes of all time should he fall to the "unstoppable" Abdul-Jabbar. Few professional sports teams in history, if any, were ever under this kind of a microscope.

One player who was just glad to be there was McMillian, a second-year forward who had become a fan favorite. Round one saw the Chicago Bulls. They were no threat and fell in four, but who cares? Kareem rode into town like Heinz Guderian during the blitzkrieg. The best sportswriter who ever lived, Jim Murray, regularly doled out those kinds of grandiose military references. He wrote like that, and this was a grand stage for him, a drama worthy of the Greeks or the Bard himself. Attempts to write using Murray's kind of language are pure homage at best, with full acknowledgment that he cannot be duplicated.

The first game of the 1972 Western Conference Finals between Milwaukee and Los Angeles at the Forum was so full of angst, pain, despair, dread, and, to use the term of another great writer, *fear and loathing* as to be almost beyond description. There are few games that have ever matched it.

Oh, how to describe it? Casey striking out? No, that's not big enough. Think more like the Federals throwing down their weapons at Bull Run, turning and running to the horror of Union sympathizers lined up in the countryside to observe the

NUMBERS DON'T LIE (OR DO THEY?)

The Lakers' 2,848–1,799 all-time regular-season record (entering 2007–08) is the greatest in NBA history. In addition to their 14 championships, they have lost in the Finals 14 times.

proceedings in picnic splendor. David versus Goliath? Well, there were two Goliaths, and the younger one, in the name of Kareem Abdul-Jabbar, rode astride the basketball world in a way that somebody more eloquent than this author—think of Phillip Roth in *The Great American Novel* perhaps—might have been able to adequately describe.

The *greatest team of all time*, playing at home before the fawning celebrityhood of "Los Angeleez," came out to meet the defending champs. There was Abdul-Jabbar, who in person represented an awesome presence. His talents were even more mind-boggling than the above-the-dugout view of Nolan Ryan's heater at its most blazing or Joe Montana's sideline manipulation in the closing minutes.

Basketball offers this kind of up-close-and-personal experience. There they are, a few feet away, unhidden by masks and helmets, their faces grimaced, their grunts heard, the swish of the basket reaching into the consciousness amid the squeal of sneaker on wood, coach yelling, fans imploring.

There are few experiences that can match that of the truly disappointing home game. The players wake up, and each moment is preparation as they eat, dress, drive to the Forum, greet the security guards, warm up, prepare, hear the building avalanche of crowd noise, and then...

Abdul-Jabbar: just a few years earlier he had been one of their own, doing astounding things at UCLA. Plenty of people at the Forum that day had sat in the Pauley Pavilion stands and seen then–Lew Alcindor swat blocks, dunk dunks. They knew, they *knew* how awesome he was. He had demonstrated it in the streak-buster in Wisconsin. All the dread stored up in the back of the minds of the Lakers faithful just poured out, like tears when a really good psychiatrist hits just the right emotional buttons.

After all the hype, the psychoses of the thing, the final score was Bucks 93, Lakers 72. This looks like just a final score, but it is not. Los Angeles had been held below 100 just once during the regular season. In the third period of Game 1 they scored eight points. A basketball game, when it becomes a rout, takes on a track-meet quality. That is what this looked like—the Bucks streaking up the court, popping baskets, Abdul-Jabbar dunking in front of Chamberlain like an enemy soldier torturing the horseless Richard III.

The crowd, the celebrity *crowd*, by the fourth quarter had abandoned their charges in favor of the San Diego Freeway and recriminations. In light of this team's history, the baggage could have filled an airport terminal. And of course, *what about poor Jerry?*

So it was that the Bucks and Lakers got set to play Game 2. The crowd settled in, this time more like witnesses at San Quentin. Bill Sharman faced a challenge like few basketball coaches have ever faced. He had been coaching in San Francisco and Utah while all this angst was taking place in Tinseltown. His natural ego had convinced him throughout training camp and the pitiable little regular season that he could *motivate Wilt...install a new offense...*but that was all normal stuff. This was not normal. This was the indomitable Kareem and the playoffs, when fundamentals go out the window. This was opening night on Broadway, face-to-face with the Desert Fox at El Alamein—there was just no *preparation* for this kind of pressure.

Game 2, Forum: Jerry West, turning his hand, shot just 10 of 30. The Bucks ran the floor, scoring at will.

Jim McMillian...the pudgy forward saved the team's *history* that night with 42 points. By the thinnest of margins, by the barest of bare one-point victories, the Lakers somehow managed to escape with a 135–134 win.

On to Milwaukee. The Bucks: 61 percent from the floor. Abdul-Jabbar: 33 points. But Chamberlain crowded him, playing the greatest defensive quarter of his career to hold the Bucks supercenter scoreless the final 11 minutes. Goodrich poured in 30,

McMillian 27, and the Lakers actually led the series after the 108–105 win, two games to one. The Rubicon had been crossed.

Game 4: perhaps the Lakers strategy was to identify the games they would lose and simply provide no effort, therefore giving their opponents false hope while giving themselves much-needed mental and physical rest from the rigors of actually *trying*. So it seemed in the 114–88 blowout loss—another below-100 effort— with Abdul-Jabbar leading the way with 31. After the game, West made the incongruous complaint that Cooke required him to *play too many minutes*. This statement from *Jerry West!*

Game 5, Los Angeles: West was again so frustrated by his failure to score that he threw a fit, during and after the game. In spite of that, it was as if the basketball gods were righting all the past wrongs: West's teammates were *finally* picking up the slack, this time in the form of a 115–90 blowout. Afterward, West was in unfamiliar territory, complaining about the press's coverage of his slump—as if in the past nobody had noticed that he was superhuman in defeat. The man was so consumed by his personal responsibility that the fact that his team was one win away from a monumental victory over Kareem Abdul-Jabbar seemed to escape his attention.

Sharman came up with the perfect observation, which was that it was West's *defense* that had won the game, and that defense, ranging from empire building to basketball, is the key to victory.

Game 6, Milwaukee: after all the frustration and angst, the possibility that Los Angeles would triumph over the almighty Bucks had a surreal quality to it, but it was wrapped around the historical knowledge that this franchise had been there before, only to fail time and time again.

Instead of folding, however, Sharman's men won a hard-fought 104–100 road victory, and it was on to the Finals, which of course added to the drama. Abdul-Jabbar & Co. represented a challenge perhaps even greater than Russell's Celtics. The mission was accomplished, but it had been in the conference finals, not the NBA Finals. The chance to fail presented itself on the world's biggest stage: New York City.

The Knickerbockers were overachievers. By any standard of sports prediction, this Lakers team could not lose, but Game 1 was a duplicate of the first playoff contest with Milwaukee. At the Forum, Los Angeles failed in utterly miserable style. It was incredible that a team this good, that scored at the pace they were scoring, could be this bad. New York beat them as if they were a pro squad and the Lakers a collegiate outfit, 114–92. The home crowd was making its way to the parking lot in the third quarter, early even by L.A. standards. Dejection was the order of the day.

Here we go again.

West was beside himself. So close, and yet so far. If this team lost to *these guys*, it would overwhelm all previous disappointments. It could not be. It would be too unbearable.

"Each of the previous Finals, they were overcome with a sense that fortune had turned against them," wrote Roland Lazenby in *The Lakers: A Basketball Journey.* But "dame fortune" was turned around by Happy Hairston in Game 2, when his 12 second-half points spurred a 106–92 pasting. Afterward, for the very first time, West allowed himself to start thinking about the NBA championship, and how he would react to it.

In Game 3, Los Angeles exploded to an easy 107–96 win.

The key was Game 4 at Madison Square Garden. Chamberlain injured his wrist but played through it. It went into overtime, the New York crowd in a frenzy. Chamberlain was in foul trouble, but he refused to play like it, blocking key shots to fuel the 116–111 Lakers win that took the air out of the crowd and the Knicks, sending the series back to Los Angeles amid palpable excitement.

Chamberlain shone with 24 points and 29 rebounds in a dominating MVP performance, fueling a total 114–100 runaway that had the Forum faithful beside themselves.

The celebration, however, was muted. L.A. fans did not charge the floor in the manner of the East Coast fans of that era. There were no balloons, as in 1969. In the dressing room, the team celebrated quietly, with none of the raucous craziness that marks most world championships.

They sipped champagne, not out of the bottle, but out of glasses. They did not pour it all over themselves. Cooke came in, all smiles. Sharman was relieved. West was totally relieved. Wilt was reserved. They were champions of the world. Finally.

Cooke, the man who would be king, should have known from his studies of empires that glory is fleeting. The "curse" seemed to return with a vengeance over the next few years. Sharman's wife died of cancer, and with his voice destroyed he had to get out of coaching. Cooke himself suffered a massive heart attack. Chamberlain and West were old and had little left in the tank. There was just enough for one last hurrah, however.

They won 60 regular-season games in 1972–73 and beat Golden State, who had upset Kareem's Bucks, in the playoffs. The Knicks were waiting again after winning one of the all-time great series with Boston.

MEDIA MONSTERS

No sooner did the players shower, dress, and take off for the postgame party after winning the 1972 NBA title than a controversy arose over the size of their winning bonuses, which were paltry. The players decided that instead of accepting the $1,500 bonuses, they would pool them together and give it all to Bill Sharman. Jack Kent Cooke then got Melvin Durslag of the *Los Angeles Herald-Examiner* to write a false story that the players, instead of giving Sharman their money, were conspiring to cut his share.

Durslag had a reputation as a hack who could be bought off. In 1960 he wrote a controversial "explanation to my friends" article on behalf of blacklisted baseball manager Leo Durocher, which had the effect of causing the Dodgers to hire Durocher as a "celebrity coach." Durocher, an utterly amoral man, spent four years conspiring to undermine manager Walter Alston and take his job. His number one hatchet man was Durslag, who infuriated the usually reserved Alston. Alston finally confronted Durslag, telling him, "You seem so concerned about Durocher's feelings, what about mine?"

"Whenever he wanted something derogatory written about me or Wilt," said West, a man of integrity, "he got Durslag to do it."

John Havlicek and center Dave Cowens had the Celtics bound for glory, winning an incredible 68 games. Then the Knicks took it to them in the playoffs, cruising to a 3–1 series lead. Havlicek put on a heroic display in willing his team back to a 3–3 tie with the final game at home. New York somehow reversed all the momentum and won, advancing to the Finals and a rematch with Los Angeles. It seemed to be a perfect opportunity for L.A. to win a repeat and establish itself as a dynasty. At the very least, it would have been a good way to close out the era, because at their age they had reached the end of the line. The curtain came too early for their liking; the Knicks exploded and beat them in five games.

THE PLAYER

Dr. Jerry Buss is an American success story, a uniquely Western American success story. On the East Coast, there was always a sense that old money, family connections, and traditional Wharton business methods were the formula to success.

The 1849 California gold rush changed all that. Eastern failures could reinvent themselves out West. Old money was no greener than new money. In the West, land speculation, entrepreneurial capitalism, and new ideas were allowed to flourish. It was this way of thinking that spurred Jerry Buss toward the attainment of his dreams. Jack Kent Cooke wanted people to think he was a blue-blood aristocrat; Buss embraced the fact that he was not.

Buss grew up disadvantaged in Southern California and then moved to the big-sky country of Wyoming. His stepfather treated him poorly. The family fell into poverty. He broke the rules but always made good grades.

Buss dropped out of high school, worked odd jobs, and then returned to get his diploma. Told by his counselors that he had academic skills, he went to the University of Wyoming, where he excelled. He decided to expand his horizons in Los Angeles, returning to the land of his youth. Buss earned a PhD in chemistry from the University of Southern California and went to work in the aerospace industry. This is a sector of the Los Angeles economy virtually invented by Howard Hughes. It stretches roughly from Westchester to Long Beach along the I-405 Corridor. Buss used his education, credentials, and experience to land a professorship at USC.

At USC, Buss followed the Trojan football team with intense enthusiasm. He and his pal Hampton Mears went to every game. Buss dreamed of owning a sports franchise. He constantly strategized on how to use his skills in the marketing of a successful sports operation. Deciding to become an entrepreneur, a natural for somebody with his background, Buss began to buy real estate in Southern California at just the right time: while he could still afford it. Selling it made him a millionaire. Married with four children, he divorced and became a player in the swingin' Southern California singles scene. His reputation as a playboy grew, as did his real estate empire.

In 1974 Buss entered professional sports as the owner of the L.A. Strings of World Team Tennis. That venture failed, but it did fuel his desire to own a major franchise. In 1975 he began to negotiate with Jack Kent Cooke, beginning with a cooperative effort between the two to promote the Strings at the Forum. Over the next few years Cooke and Buss talked about Cooke's professed desire to sell the Forum. Cooke did not really want to sell, but in the late 1970s he was going through what eventually became a record-setting divorce, forcing him to liquidate his holdings.

"There were times when I felt I'd gotten in a little over my head," said Buss. "Jack Kent Cooke is remarkably charming when he wants to be, and he's a very, very tough-willed man. He may have the toughest will I've ever seen. It's like iron. And he was very quick to take advantage of turns in the negotiations."

As Cooke's settlement negotiations got out of hand, he realized he needed to sell everything in order to satisfy the greed of his wife and her divorce lawyers. Everything he had worked for, all he had accomplished—he would not be allowed to keep it.

A complicated agreement involving the Forum, the Lakers and Kings, Buss's real estate holdings, and the Chrysler Building in New York, apparently "thrown in" to soften the tax blow, was worked out. But Cooke always came up with a twist at the last

Dr. Jerry Buss is the embodiment of millions of people who have looked to California to reach for the stars and struck gold. Photo courtesy of Bettmann/CORBIS.

minute, which was a negotiating tactic of his. First, he wanted to sell his ranch in the Sierra Nevadas, and then Buss had to scramble for an additional $2.7 million to cover the Chrysler Building.

It was about a $70 million deal and one of the most complicated financial transactions in U.S. history. Reporters and accountants tried to track down the money but could not do it. It involved 15 or 20 limited partnerships, real estate transactions and sales, plenty of "other people's money," and a lot of lawyers.

It was the kind of deal that Cooke thrived on. He seemed to have gotten the best of it. Buss may well have been in over his head. In order to make it succeed from his end of the bargain, he would have to oversee successful operations of the Lakers, Kings, and the Forum. In this respect, his vision, hard work, and perhaps a little bit of luck paid off. He enjoyed wild success beyond anything Cooke—who was no failure—had experienced.

Buss oversaw the Showtime Lakers. He eventually sold the Kings but made the franchise successful enough to eventually lure Wayne Gretzky to L.A. He initiated many marketing ventures. His deal to change the Forum to the Great Western Forum, for better or worse, started the trend of naming stadiums after corporations.

He also was an innovative champion of cable sports television. Prime Ticket begat Fox Sports, the expansion of ESPN, and all their variations. Buss maintained a strong affiliation with USC. His daughter, Jeanie Buss, graduated from USC and followed in her father's footsteps with the Lakers, where she became an executive vice president.

Buss started another trend, in that he was one of the first "playboy owners," an open-shirt and jeans guy known for having beautiful women around him long before the Maloof brothers and other sports owners of that stripe.

STADIUM STORIES

THE FORUM

According to legend, Jack Kent Cooke was having a meeting with a city bureaucrat named Ernest Debs. In response to Cooke's request for a publicly financed facility for his basketball and hockey operations, Debs basically laughed in his face. At that point, Cooke announced that he was scouting locations for an arena built out of his private fortune.

"*Har, har, har,*" Debs smirked.

"He didn't laugh," Cooke recalled. "He said the words *har, har, har.*"

This bureaucrat may have mocked him, but Cooke got the last laugh.

"Let's depart this den of iniquity," he told his lawyers.

They drove straight to the office of the architectural firm Charles Luckman Associates, who had recently upgraded the new Madison Square Garden in New York City.

The original drawings did not meet Cooke's approval, so he directed the architect not to think about the future, but rather the past, as in "two thousand years and six thousand miles east of here," said Cooke.

Cooke wanted something out of Caesar's Rome or Plato's Greece. A *forum*. With columns. He never wanted the place to be called an *arena*. He wanted it to be a brand name: the Forum, or better yet, the "*Fabulous* Forum."

85

When Chick Hearn said the idea was, well, "fabulous," it was like the Mercury space program: all systems go! When he indeed built the "Fabulous Forum," which opened for business in 1967–68, it was an instant success. Like Dodger Stadium, the Forum was immediately the finest facility in its sport by leaps and bounds. It was as beautiful as Pauley Pavilion was when it opened in 1965, but the Forum was more spectacular. Nobody had ever seen anything like it. Musty old gyms throughout the country were utterly desolate in comparison. It was so tremendous that for years, perhaps decades, no arena built after it even compared. Not until America West Arena (now US Airways Arena) in Phoenix opened in 1992 did the NBA start to see facilities that could match it.

The Forum also had the effect, unfortunately for USC and the Sports Arena, of immediately changing perceptions of that facility. Considered a top-notch college arena, as good as most of the pro venues, suddenly the Sports Arena became, like Candlestick Park in San Francisco, seemingly old and decrepit overnight.

People also started to take note that the neighborhood surrounding USC and the Sports Arena was dangerous, especially at night. When Cooke underwent construction of the Forum in Inglewood—located a few miles southwest of downtown L.A. and

The late, great L.A. Forum, with its distinctive shape and columns, was deliberately designed and named after its ancient predecessors in Rome and Greece at the behest of the Lakers' modern-day Caesar, Jack Kent Cooke.

RIVALRIES

Entering the 2007–08 season, the Lakers were 77–24 versus Phoenix at home, but only 39–61 against the Suns on the road (116–85 overall).

triangulated between what is now the 110, 105, and 405 freeways, next to Hollywood Park Racetrack—it was still considered a white, blue-collar suburb. Police officers and tech workers at the nearby aerospace plants that dot Howard Hughes's L.A. from Westchester to Long Beach still lived there.

Inglewood in those days associated itself with the South Bay, the upscale beach communities of Manhattan, Hermosa, Redondo, and adjacent Torrance. Nearby Hawthorne High School was in fact the home of the Beach Boys, whose music dominated the L.A. music scene of that time and place. The looming hills of the exclusive Palos Verdes Peninsula looked, by L.A. standards of distance at least, to be part of the neighborhood.

In 1965, however, violent riots broke out in Watts. Suddenly, the distance between Watts and Inglewood looked a lot closer to the blue-collar whites who lived there. They moved—"white flight," they called it—to Orange County, to the San Fernando Valley, to the Inland Empire. They left the neighborhood around the Forum to the tender mercies of encroaching south-central Los Angeles. By the end of the 1960s, Inglewood was part of what might be called "Greater Compton," and this is not an endearing term.

Despite the deterioration of the neighborhood, however, the Forum, like USC, would be an island of class and wealth amidst a sea of poverty and crime. Los Angelenos were used to driving through mean streets on their way to and from sporting events at the Coliseum and the Forum.

The Forum was also convenient. Freeway construction made it accessible for people from all areas of the L.A. Basin, whether it be downtown, the Westside, the valley, the beaches, Long Beach, or Orange County.

It was opened just 18 months after groundbreaking. The folks over at the Sports Arena Commission rooted against it, calling it "Cooke's folly." Cooke had looked at a number of sites in L.A. proper and in the San Fernando Valley before settling on the 29-acre site at the corner of Manchester and Prairie Avenues.

The Philadelphia Spectrum was built at about the same time, at a cost of $5 million. The Spectrum never compared to the $16 million Forum. Cooke wanted everything to be first class. Each of the 80 columns supporting the roof, which stood 57 feet high, weighed 55 tons. The columns were so huge they had to be created on the work site instead of shipped in.

Construction crews worked double shifts because Cooke's hockey team, the Kings, needed the building in order to make their NHL debut. Cooke's vision of hockey in L.A. was a wonder in and of itself. In warm-weather Los Angeles, a city essentially built on a desert, ice hockey seemed to be a distant concept, but Cooke knew that many Canadians and easterners lived in the area, with more moving in all the time. Eventually, the Kings would be a marquee team in the city, with the California Golden Seals, the Anaheim Mighty Ducks, and the San Jose Sharks following in their footsteps.

In Cooke's mind he was like Caesar, overseeing the gladiatorial games of the ancient Roman Colosseum. He wanted regal ambience fit for a king; or a ruler, which is how he saw himself. What this says about him is questionable. He was a man who lived in modern America, with all the rules, laws, and constraints that decent society places on its men of power, so any conjecture about what Cooke may have thought to be within the realm of his powers had he reigned in ancient Rome or over some fiefdom must remain speculation.

BY THE NUMBERS

14—the total number of championships won by the Lakers in Minneapolis and Los Angeles between 1949 and 2002. Boston has 16.

MEDIA MONSTERS

Fox Sports has a popular bar/restaurant located in the STAPLES Center that is open every day.

But Cooke saw the Forum to be an extension of Hollywood opulence. That meant comfort, wealth, and a sense of sexiness that would become as much a trademark of the Lakers image as any team in sports. He wanted beautiful actresses and matinee idols to be seen at his Forum. He built fully upholstered, extra-wide, theater-style seats, with rows spaced to provide legroom—all novel concepts at the time—to accommodate the rich and famous.

Cooke knew that a certain advantage was to be had in an indoor facility, especially one that housed winter sports. Weather would not affect the comfort or style of the patrons, who could attend events at the Forum dressed to impress. He wanted the games to resemble a Hollywood premiere.

On December 30, 1967, the Forum opened with a hockey game between the Kings and the Philadelphia Flyers. His old friend and mentor, Lord Thomson, attended. The master of ceremonies was *Bonanza* star Lorne Greene.

The next night, after the Forum crew worked efficiently to convert the floor for basketball, the Lakers beat the San Diego Rockets (featuring a young player named Pat Riley), 147–118.

A press release stated that the Forum would "be in essence a modern version of the greater Colosseum of ancient Rome."

The Lakers' new uniforms, entirely designed by Cooke, featured the color purple, but Cooke instructed announcer Chick Hearn to call it "Forum blue, so don't adjust your TV sets."

The gold background was groundbreaking. It was the first time a home team did not wear white. Ushers were dressed in togas. Female employees, chosen for physical attractiveness, were outfitted in Las Vegas–style cocktail dresses with a Roman motif. The whole scene resembled Caesar's Palace in Las Vegas, which was built one year earlier. Cooke actively courted celebrities. Walter Matthau and Jack Nicholson were on board from the beginning.

JEWEL OF THE DOWNTOWN CORRIDOR

STAPLES Center opened in the fall of 1999 and quickly came to be recognized as the best of all NBA basketball arenas, but it is far more than that. STAPLES represents two things: the revitalization of Los Angeles sports and, just as important, the rejuvenation of downtown Los Angeles.

In 1880, the University of Southern California opened for business a few blocks to the south of where STAPLES is now located. At the time, it was in the fanciest neighborhood in the city. After World War I, downtown Los Angeles became a thriving business center.

But as the movie industry expanded, studios and related businesses needed open space to create lots and to film. A sense of separation between the traditional downtown businesses—law, banking, oil—and the new—agents, publicists, advertising—created a physical separation.

After ground was broken to build UCLA, the land west of Western Avenue was quickly developed. Beverly Hills became a fashionable city of mansions, boutiques, and showbiz. Santa Monica and the beach cities, once considered vacation resorts, became connected to Los Angeles by the 10 Freeway. The Westside became all the rage. Downtown lost its panache.

In the 1990s L.A. took major hits in the form of a riot, loss of political power, the O.J. scandal, an earthquake, and the longest dry spell ever for all levels of its sports teams. But two beacons of hope shone forth. For one thing, the air became much cleaner. Thanks to the automotive industry creating cleaner-burning fuel, a new, bright day emerged. There was

DID YOU KNOW...

That in 1967–68, the Lakers hired Al Michaels, then in his twenties, as Chick Hearn's color analyst?

The sparkling STAPLES Center, part of a revitalized L.A. downtown, has been home to the Lakers since 1999 and was anointed with three-straight NBA titles by Shaq, Kobe, and Phil.

a time when, aside from rare winter days right after a rain, fans on one side of the Coliseum could barely see the other side. The Hollywood sign, the San Gabriel Mountains, they were like the Holy Ghost. It was there, but you could not see it. By the late 1990s, however, the beautiful downtown panoramas of the L.A. Basin revealed themselves in all their splendor.

The second thing that happened was that under Mayor Richard Riordan, a major downtown gentrification project was undertaken. Crime was reduced. New condos, museums, skyscrapers, and nightlife replaced old buildings.

When the STAPLES Center went up, it seemed to be in symbolic confluence with the new millennium that began a few months later. A combination of architecture and sports success has worked hand in hand ever since.

"BORN IN THE U.S.A."

The first event ever held at the STAPLES Center was Bruce Springsteen and the E Street Band performing on October 17, 1999.

The Lakers of Shaquille O'Neal, Kobe Bryant, and coach Phil Jackson opened the new arena with three straight NBA titles, a feat not even Magic and Kareem had accomplished. Just down the street, USC's football team also began an unprecedented run of excellence. There seems to be a direct correlation between these two neighboring sports dynasties.

The Coliseum, one of the oldest stadiums in America, was spruced up with new scoreboards and a new sound system; and with sellout crowds a modern sense of celebration enveloped Exposition Park, the USC campus, its neighborhood, and downtown. USC bought up surrounding land, starting a gentrification project of its own. They built faculty and student housing, revitalized local schools, beautified old Victorians, and generally created a safer, cleaner, better place not just for the college but for the community.

Then USC built the Galen Center, which opened for the Trojan basketball team to rave reviews in 2006. The corridor between STAPLES and the Galen Center, roughly paralleling Figueroa Street for about a two-to-four-mile stretch, has and continues to see rebirth, with more and more nightlife, restaurants, clubs, entertainment, and good business replacing poverty.

THE GOOD, THE BAD, AND THE UGLY

JUST LIKE ANY OTHER SEVEN-FOOT BLACK MILLIONAIRE WHO LIVES NEXT DOOR

In the entire history of sports, few if any athletes have garnered the kind of response—from fans, media, teammates, opponents, critics, and supporters—that Wilt Chamberlain has.

He was called "Big Norman" by his friends, but his public monikers were "Wilt the Stilt" and "the Big Dipper." Perhaps only Babe Ruth, who dominated baseball in his day as Chamberlain did basketball in his, had as many handles: "Babe," "the Sultan of Swat," "the Bambino." Chamberlain hated the term "Wilt the Stilt." He was the ultimate big man, and especially in his era big men were seen less as people and more like giants. They were ungainly, uncoordinated, maybe a bit dumb, kind of oafish. A popular TV show of the era, *The Addams Family*, featured a huge butler named "Lurch," and this became the derogatory term applied to all big men.

Chamberlain probably did more for the image of big men than anybody before him, if not since him. He broke just about every stereotype that could be applied to athletes, seven-footers, and black males (while perpetuating a few at the same time). He later wrote a book that mocked his gaping celebrity with the title *Wilt: Just Like Any Other Seven-Foot Black Millionaire Who Lives Next Door*.

Chamberlain was a conservative Republican who unapologetically backed Richard Nixon. He was one of the first really big men

Wilt Chamberlain had the size, strength, and will to defy stereotypes and became one of the truly transcendent athletes in sports history.

WILTISMS

"Beauty is only skin-deep and ugliness goes to the bone. When beauty wears away, ugliness holds its own."
—Wilt Chamberlain's mother, quoted in A View from Above

who was not thin, viewed as somehow frail, able to be intimidated by elbows and rough play. His strength was legendary. Later he made a movie, *Conan the Barbarian,* with Arnold Schwarzenegger. Arnold expressed amazement at Wilt's strength. He could bench press as much as Arnold and do sit-ups with more weights resting on his stomach than the bodybuilder could.

Chamberlain had Ruthian sexual appetites, which he later described in a controversial book, *A View from Above*, which nobody could quite figure out. At a time in which AIDS was a very hot topic and people were convinced that it was as much a "straight" disease as a gay one (this being around the time of Magic Johnson's disclosure), he claimed an enormous number of partners. Amateur statisticians began to do the math, trying to figure out if Wilt's claims could be valid—"knocking off" conquests at the rate of several per day (one every three or four waking hours, basically) over years in which he was in school, playing basketball, practicing, traveling, eating, and, in theory, sleeping.

Chamberlain was criticized for not embracing "black causes," and he heard it from all sides because his taste in women ran the gamut: white, black, Latino, Asian, you name it. This meant he could offend just about everybody, from Christians to social conservatives to women's libbers to white racists to black racists, and everybody in between.

He provided vivid sexual descriptions of making love to women under five feet tall, causing startling mental images of crushed, naked girls, but claimed that in bed "we're all the same size."

Chamberlain was not the old-style center who blocked shots, grabbed rebounds, or made short baskets based solely on his height. His height and strength was matched by great athletic ability. Unlike many seven-footers before him, Chamberlain was as coordinated and agile as a guard. A very telling example of his athleticism was that he never fouled out of games. Big men tended to play like a "bull in a china shop," roughing up and getting roughed up until foul trouble inevitably followed. Not so with Chamberlain. He was fouled a lot, though he never mastered free throws. A decent shooter from the floor over and above his dunks and close-in layups, he was psyched out by the free throw line.

His athletic talent was so great that had he decided to play football, he most likely could have been a professional tight end or lineman, and in fact Kansas City's Hank Stram tried to get him to do just that. There was talk of a boxing match with Muhammad Ali. He probably would have been a pretty good defensive first baseman who could swing the bat, albeit protecting an enormous strike zone. He was in fact a world-class high jumper, and before joining the NBA, he was a creditable member of the Harlem Globetrotters, a team that required its players to display ultimate agility and athletic coordination in order to perform all the tricks of the trade.

In later years, Chamberlain became a regular in the ultracompetitive world of beach volleyball, making the scene by the Santa Monica Pier. His Bentley was a regular sight. Bikini-clad maidens made his acquaintance by the bushel.

Being black was as much a part of Wilt's persona as any other factor, but he did not conform to the expectations of his day. His political conservatism made him attractive to whites, of course, but then he dismayed them with his sexual proclivities and wild lifestyle. Chamberlain was a fairly good-looking fellow. He wore clothes well. There was none of the stoop-shouldered look that other too-tall men displayed, as if they were ashamed of their height. Chamberlain paraded it.

However, while Wilt loved the night life, made the club scene, was a regular at the *Playboy* mansion, stayed out all night, and liked to sleep in all day, he was never a drug user or big drinker.

At the time, African American athletes were supposed to be Christian family men, but that did not fit his profile. He also was

NUMBERS DON'T LIE (OR DO THEY?)

Entering the 2007–08 season, the Lakers' 133–167 (.443) road playoff record is the best in NBA history, ahead of Boston's 97–135 (.418) mark.

on the scene when African Americans were becoming militant, radical, and political. Bill Russell became a fierce voice for the "new breed" of militant black activist that found its way into the sports pantheon of the late 1960s, but he expressed great frustration that his "friend" Chamberlain would have nothing to do with the Stokely Carmichael, Panther wing of black politics.

This led some to think Wilt chose to stay out of radical politics because he was dumb, but he very well may have possessed the IQ of a genius. His taste in music, books, films, and culture were eclectic to the point of true intellectualism.

Chamberlain was a groundbreaker in the realm of sports economics. The $100,000 mark was considered a plateau of sorts when he emerged. As the 1960s became the 1970s, some players like Sandy Koufax, Willie Mays, and others were making around $120,000 per year. A form of "free agency" that arose out of the AFL-NFL war created some bonuses as high as $400,000 for players like Joe Namath. Boxers were on the verge of making big money, too, but basketball did not have the television deals, the stadium capacity, enough games, or the panache to generate this sort of income even among its greatest stars.

The entrance of executives like Jack Kent Cooke, the creation of palaces such as the Forum, and the excitement generated by high-profile superstars like Wilt Chamberlain helped usher the NBA into an era of economic boom. Before the big free agents escalated salaries in baseball, Chamberlain was making an astounding half-million dollars a year.

This allowed him to buy the ultimate bachelor's pad in the Hollywood Hills. It was famed for his huge bed and *boudoir* worthy of an Arabian sultan's harem. Chamberlain had a swimming pool that was half indoors, half outdoors. Whether or not he approached the numbers he bragged about in his 1991 book, *A View from Above*, it seems likely that Wilt did his share of entertaining. Magic Johnson became a ladies' man of the first order, but before him there was Wilt, and like almost everything Wilt did, he did it bigger than anybody.

"I really feel I am one of the most misunderstood celebrities of the century," Chamberlain stated in 1991. "The misunderstandings come about because of my size, my demeanor, my race, the media. For some inexplicable reason, people assume they know me and what I think and feel."

No matter what anybody thought, Chamberlain was indeed a "gentle giant." The lack of fouls assessed against him reflected the way he lived his life. Despite all the women, there were never allegations of wrongdoing or violence. Despite standing out wherever he went, moving about in a world where low-rent people no doubt wanted to challenge him and take a shot at him, there was never any history of fighting or lawbreaking.

Nevertheless, try as he might, Chamberlain remained misunderstood until the end. Maybe he thought his 1991 book would clear things up, but the controversy surrounding his claim of sexual conquests, which would make a porn star blush, served only to add to the misunderstanding.

Nobody knew quite how to respond. The sheer numbers were so outrageous that they cost doubt on his veracity, but if indeed he had been with that many women, then his morality and common sense came into question. How many children had been born out of wedlock? How many abortions? What about diseases? Chamberlain claimed all his women were single, or at least to the best of his knowledge.

MADE TO BE BROKEN

On April 11, 1967, Wilt Chamberlain blocked 17 shots in a playoff win over Bill Russell's Celtics.

"I have always believed there is more than one true love for a person," Chamberlain wrote in *A View from Above*. "I also believe that lust is more a natural part of us than love, and that one can spend every waking moment falling in and out of lust. There are a few of us who are fortunate enough to be in a position to fulfill our lustful desires. I'm one of those lucky ones. So don't be shocked to hear that if I had to count my sexual encounters, I would be closing in on twenty thousand women. Yes, that's correct, *twenty thousand different ladies*. At my age, that equals out to having sex with 1.2 women a day, every day, since I was 15 years old."

In a world of Davids, Wilt was Goliath. "And nobody roots for Goliath," he once exclaimed.

Wilt grew up in the Philadelphia projects. He played at Overbrook High School, where he once scored 60 points in a single quarter in which the opponents ran a stall. By the time he left high school, he was the greatest prep sensation in history. The NBA wanted him right out of high school and he was ready, but the rules forbade it.

An enormous recruiting battle was waged for his collegiate services. No doubt a fair number of NCAA rules were broken during this process and later when he was a student at Kansas University. Despite zone defenses designed to put as many as four men around him under the basket, Chamberlain dominated college play.

As a sophomore he scored 30 points with 19 rebounds and nine blocked shots a game. KU was the best team in the nation, but questions about Chamberlain's effectiveness within the team structure, which dogged him throughout his career, first cropped up when the Jayhawks lost in the NCAA Finals to North Carolina in three overtimes.

Chamberlain swatted blocked shots into the stands, giving the ball back to the opponent instead of handling it and passing it to a teammate. He made a big production of rebounds, smacking the ball into his hands to make a big noise instead of firing an outlet pass to start the fast break. He wanted to slow down the pace, giving himself a chance to meander on down the court, set up, receive the ball, and score.

At USF, Bill Russell was shorter and less dominant, but he would brush his blocked shots to teammates and fire outlets on the break. The Dons won 60 straight games and two national titles that way.

Chamberlain was a national-class high jumper for the Kansas track team, later lamenting that he never pursued an Olympic decathlon, which he thought he had the ability to win. He was a fast runner, never seemed to tire, possessed massive strength, and could jump high and far; he may have been a gold medalist.

Chamberlain had enough of college after his junior year, but the rules still prevented him from going to the NBA, so he joined the Harlem Globetrotters. When his class finally graduated, Chamberlain was selected by the hometown Philadelphia Warriors, and in 1959–60 he averaged 37.6 points and 27 rebounds per game. The next year he became the first player in NBA history to shoot over 50 percent from the floor, and in 1961–62 Chamberlain scored 100 points in a game, averaging over 50 on the season.

By the mid-1960s, however, Chamberlain's gaudy scoring, rebounding, and shot-blocking statistics paled in comparison to the championship rings earned by Russell. The rivalry between these two may have been the greatest personal duel in sports history. Physically, Russell was no comparison, but he was said to have a bigger heart, a criticism that cut Chamberlain to the bone.

"He didn't give him the offensive position he wanted," said Russell's teammate, Hall of Famer Bob Cousy, of the smaller man's tactics in containing the "slower" Wilt. "Russell kept him from overpowering him and going to the basket. Russell had better speed and quickness, so he could always beat Wilt to the spot. He pushed Chamberlain out a little further from the basket, forcing him to put the ball on the floor once or twice. We always felt Russell could handle him one-on-one."

This may have been the key. By "handling" Wilt one-on-one, it freed Russell's Boston teammates to defend Wilt's less-talented teammates. Russell knew when to back off and give Chamberlain the points he could not prevent him from scoring or the rebounds he could not grab away from him. Russell took the opportunity to

CAN'T ANYBODY HERE PLAY THIS GAME?

That's what Kareem Abdul-Jabbar must have been thinking to himself in his first year with the Lakers (1975–76). Despite winning the league MVP award, the team was 40–42 with a cast of old men.

catch a breather instead of running himself ragged every second of the game. Wilt would get his numbers—40 or 50 points, 15 to 20 rebounds—but they were not the game-deciding plays his team needed to beat the Celtics. It was also true that the Celtics double- and triple-teamed him, which Chamberlain pointed out nobody ever did to Russell on the other end of the floor.

Russell would come away with nine points, maybe 17 points, maybe even a few more, but his rebounds and blocked shots were the crucial winning edge time after time. Chamberlain had the reputation of being a selfish player, obsessed with his own statistics, but Jerry West strongly disputed that notion.

"No athlete wants to fail," said West. "Wilt Chamberlain certainly did not want to."

Whether Chamberlain was selfish in his early years or not, the evidence is that in later years he was not. He won world championships with the Philadelphia 76ers and the Lakers in seasons in which his scoring averages were far below his earlier career norms, on teams in which he had talented teammates who took his assists and scored on their own. His defense and rebounding fueled those title teams.

Eventually, his *lack* of shot taking was astounding. He was a man of extremes, in almost all phases of his life and career. The truth is, he was a superstar with the Warriors and 76ers but met his match in Russell and the Celtics. It was a true "war of the worlds," won by the greater champion, Russell, but not lost because of a failure on Chamberlain's part. This was the case at least until the late 1960s when Chamberlain inexplicably seemed to give up or, some said, was concerned more about his pride or a dispute with his coach than he was about driving his team to the

QUOTATIONS

"For so long, all the attention, even the praise, was like a storm to get out."
—Kareem Abdul-Jabbar, 1990

Promised Land. This was the view held by a fair number of detractors, but the Butch van Breda Kolff benching at the end of Game 7 of the 1969 Finals against Boston seems to have occurred against Wilt's wishes.

"Chamberlain is not an easy man to love," said Franklin Mieuli, the owner of the Warriors when Wilt played for them. Two years after the Warriors moved to San Francisco, he traded Wilt back to his hometown team, the Sixers.

Wilt's frustration with Russell did not change when he donned the 76er uniform. He lost a seven-game Eastern Finals to Boston. He led Philly to the division crown over them one year, only to lose in five games in the playoffs.

In 1967 he *finally* had the supporting cast to exorcise the demons of Boston hegemony. As if relieved not to be faced with the scoring burden, he dished off to Billy Cunningham and Hal Greer all year on a remarkable 68–13 team that went on to capture the NBA championship.

People were talking about a dynasty in Philadelphia, but it all fell apart a year later when the Sixers lost in 1968 to Boston, who in turn beat the Lakers. In Los Angeles, Chamberlain found his home. It was rough at first, especially when van Breda Kolff benched him with a minor injury in the closing minutes of that terrible Game 7 loss. But the fault was correctly assigned to the coach when the truth came out. Wilt had not "sat out," as Bill Russell alleged. His knee injury the next year made him a sympathetic figure for the first time. His performance against Willis Reed again brought up questions about his heart in the 1970 Finals versus New York. When he and Jerry West led Los Angeles to a pro record 33 straight wins, a league record 69–13 mark, the NBA title, and strong consideration as the *greatest team of all time*—this being the second team he was on in five years to earn this moniker, which says a lot—all was right in the world. Wilt, finally, was a true icon of Los Angeles, up there with West and Baylor, Drysdale and Koufax, Wooden and Alcindor, Eastwood and Nicholson.

Wilt retired to a life of leisure. He grew a goatee and wore a headband toward the end of his career, which gave him a "Goliath" look on the beaches but fit in with the '70s motif. He got into bodybuilding. Always big, he became massive and made the rounds of magazine covers glistening in sweat, flexing his biceps. Chamberlain developed into a beach volleyball player of some repute and was part of the growth of that game that occurred over the next decades.

He made movies, namely with Arnold, whom he befriended and in so doing entered the bodybuilding pantheon. Arnold observed that had he gone that way Wilt could have succeeded in his sport, which, like beach volleyball, grew over the years. Wilt never married or had children (that we know about), but the tendency for males to fantasize only added to the legend that he entertained the most beautiful women in the world at his Bel Air pad. Despite the chauvinistic nature of his persona he became a true, active pioneer in the growth and promotion of women's sports in the wake of Title IX.

Chamberlain held onto his money, yet eventually the salaries he made, which were so astounding at the time, paled in comparison to the megabucks of his successors. He avoided heavy partying, but not the party scene, while maintaining an active, healthy lifestyle.

Chamberlain died much too early, in 1999, and even this was misunderstood. He did not die because he had a bad lifestyle, at least not in terms of exercise, diet, or substance abuse. It was as if the sheer weight of his body—or the weight of his whole bigger-than-life life—was too much to keep carrying around.

THE ENIGMA

Ferdinand Lewis Alcindor Jr. weighed 13 pounds when he was born on April 16, 1947. His father was a transit authority lieutenant, and his mother was 6'1". His parents were overprotective and strict disciplinarians. He grew up in the Dyckman Projects, which were in those days just beginning to seethe with increasing crime and drug activity. Alcindor's parents were determined that their son would not fall prey to such things.

"I used to get my ass handed to me on a regular basis," he said. "On the New York streets where I was growing up, if you didn't know how to fight you were in big trouble, and I just didn't have the instinct. I was always bigger than the kids my age, but there would be guys two and three years older who felt called upon to kick my ass at every opportunity. They were just bad, mean, streetwise nine-year-old boys ready to go for the kill."

Christianity was seen as the shield from temptation and bad influence. They were Roman Catholics and Alcindor attended St. Jude's School. He showed an immediate aptitude for sports but was exposed to culture in order to round out his personality. He swam, ice-skated, and played musical instruments (his father had studied trombone at Juilliard), all the while making excellent grades each step of the way.

Lew was a good baseball player in the Manhattan youth leagues, dreaming of playing for Jackie Robinson's Brooklyn Dodgers. By the time he reached the eighth grade, however, he was a 6'8" basketball *wunderkind*, recruited by prep schools throughout the East Coast. He chose Power Memorial Academy, an elite all-boys Catholic school on the West Side. At Power Memorial, Alcindor was one of the only African American kids. Power Memorial's schedule included mostly white opponents. The young man came to understand the nature of race, special treatment, and ego.

Alcindor's four varsity years at Power Memorial most likely constitute the greatest prep career ever, possibly in any sport. Alcindor reached seven feet in height as a 14-year-old freshman, the year he was first featured in a game that had to be moved to Madison Square Garden in order to accommodate the crowd. Not until LeBron James did a high school basketball player get the kind of attention Alcindor did, and Lew did not have the benefit of ESPN.

CELEBRITY CORNER

Four of Lew Alcindor's classmates at UCLA included movie director Francis Ford Coppola and three rock legends: Jim Morrison, Ray Manzarek, and John Densmore of The Doors.

Playing for coach Jack Donohue, Alcindor led Power Memorial to undefeated seasons and New York City Catholic High School championships in his sophomore and junior years.

"Most big boys are awkward," said Donohue. "But after his freshman year, you couldn't say that about Lewie any more. Sure, he was given talent. But others have had that and didn't develop it. I think Lewie's biggest asset was tremendous pride."

Alcindor conducted his first interview at age 13, learning how to "handle" the media, but his nature was quiet and shy. He studied to be an engineer, telling journalists, "I know I can't play basketball forever."

In later years, Alcindor ruffled feathers by claiming that Donohue had pressured him into attending a summer basketball camp outside the city, in order to create publicity and greater enrollment that would make money for Donohue. Alcindor claimed that he was isolated by his size and race at the camp, forced to suffer various indignities. His plight was all but ignored by the coach, according to Alcindor.

He also revealed that Donohue used the "N word" while berating him at halftime of the famed Power Memorial–DeMatha game in his senior year of 1965. The two-time national champions traveled to Washington, D.C., to take on unbeaten, second-ranked DeMatha in a game that would determine national supremacy. Alcindor said that Donohue did not do it out of racism, but rather to get him to wake up in a game in which he played poorly. Nevertheless, it stunned Alcindor and did not have the effect of inspiring him. He was held to 16 points in a stunning loss to DeMatha that made coast-to-coast headlines. Afterward, Donohue was conciliatory. Alcindor took the blame, but the coach said that

TOP CLUTCH PERFORMERS

"Big Game James" Worthy was named MVP of the 1988 Finals. The first pick of the 1982 draft, he played on three championship teams and was a seven-time All-Star. Four times he averaged over 20 points a game and was named one of the 50 Greatest Players during the NBA's 50th anniversary in 1996–97.

was unfair; he was responsible for all the victories that came before that game. Alcindor was also an excellent student and became the most highly recruited collegiate athlete ever.

"I'll trade two first-round draft picks for him right now," said Baltimore Bullets coach Gene Shue, but the rules of the day strictly prohibited that. The recruiting process was fraught with controversy. New York City considered Alcindor to be a form of "public property." Editorials urged him to play collegiate ball in the city, or at least on the East Coast. Any move to Michigan—or, even worse, California—was seen as a form of treachery.

Things heated up even more when Donohue was hired at Holy Cross, presumably with the *proviso* that he would bring Alcindor with him. Great influence was played on the youngster. He later expressed indignation at his coach's pressure tactics, implying that he "owed" it to Donohue to attend Holy Cross. Religious pressure was also brought to bear on him. Alcindor was a Roman Catholic playing at a Catholic high school. It was felt that he should continue at a Catholic university. He later revealed that he converted to Islam in his senior year at Power Memorial Academy, which would have been a major controversy had it been publicly known at the time.

Dr. Ralph Bunche, an African American basketball player at UCLA in the 1920s, had gone on to win the Nobel Peace Prize for his role in mediating a cease-fire in the wake of Israel's 1948 creation. He helped to recruit Alcindor, who was impressed with him, the beautiful UCLA campus, California weather, casual attitudes, and of course legendary coach John Wooden.

At the time that Alcindor signed with UCLA, the Bruins had just won the second of two straight NCAA titles (1964–65) and were primed to move into the gleaming new Pauley Pavilion the following season. Nobody else could compete with all that, so it was "California, here I come" for Lew Alcindor.

The very first basketball game ever played at Pauley Pavilion was an exhibition between defending national champion, number one–ranked UCLA and their freshman team, which was prevented from playing varsity ball due to existing NCAA rules. A capacity crowd watched in awe as Alcindor utterly dominated the older players, leading the frosh to a resounding 75–60 victory with 31 points.

That 1965–66 UCLA team got off to a slow start, but by year's end Wooden felt that they were the best team in the nation and would have won the NCAA Tournament. However, early-season conference losses prevented them from going, since there were no "at-large" selections at the time. It was the only Wooden team between 1964 and 1974 not to win the national championship. Texas Western's historic all–African American starting five won the NCAA title that year (over Pat Riley's Kentucky Wildcats), but there is little question that had Alcindor's freshman team played, they would have won. Of course, if they had mixed with the varsity it would have been a *fait accompli*.

Alcindor led UCLA to an 88–2 record and three straight national championships. His first game as a sophomore was against crosstown rival Southern California. Alcindor scored 56 in a crushing win. He scored 61 against Washington State.

"No matter how good many of the Bruins are," wrote Frank Deford in *Sports Illustrated*, "and how well they are coached by John Wooden, their game is Lew Alcindor...Alcindor's influence is so pervasive that it is difficult to determine how good his teammates really are."

Opponents used zones, to no avail. The NCAA outlawed the dunk. Nothing could stop him. He scored 30 points with 15 rebounds a game to lead the unbeaten Bruins to the national championship as a sophomore. It was only Wooden's team concept that prevented him from scoring at will, breaking all records. Elvin Hayes and Houston managed to beat Alcindor's Bruins when Big Lew played with a bandage on his eye after a finger had been poked in it. In the rematch, UCLA absolutely annihilated the Cougars in the NCAA Tournament. USC had defeated the Bruins using a stall in the regular season, but the team never lost in the tournament. Alcindor was a three-time tournament Most Outstanding Player, a three-time national Player of the Year, the leading scorer in UCLA history, and, at the time of his graduation with a B average, the sixth leading scorer in collegiate history. There was a sense that Wooden dictated the score of UCLA's games, with a tendency to hold the numbers down for the sake of fairness to Alcindor's teammates as well as their opponents.

Wooden placed a strict moratorium on player interviews. The purpose was to prevent Alcindor from getting all the attention, but it also kept his deserving teammates from getting publicity. Alcindor's exclusive story, written for *Sports Illustrated* after graduation, and an intriguing 1973 book, *The Wizard of Westwood*, written by *L.A. Times* reporters Dwight Chapin and Jeff Prugh, revealed some of the angst that always seemed to shadow Alcindor's façade, however.

At the time, he was portrayed as a happy, intelligent black kid who had found paradise in race-neutral California, but as with all things the truth was more complicated. Cassius Clay had recently evaded the draft and changed his name to Muhammad Ali, in accordance with his conversion to Islam. Alcindor revealed in *Sports Illustrated* that throughout his college career he was a closet Muslim. His new name was Kareem Abdul-Jabbar, although he did not officially go by that until 1971.

In *The Wizard of Westwood*, a conversation among Alcindor, his teammates, and Coach Wooden, which took place on a train delayed by a blizzard outside of Chicago, described Lew denying the divinity of Jesus Christ and the role of America in the world. Wooden, a devout Christian, was appalled, but in accord with his gentle demeanor handled the situation in a calm manner.

"Just because we disagree," Wooden said, "does not mean we have to be disagreeable."

BUSINESS COMES FIRST

"Now I know I should have left my feelings to myself," Magic Johnson said of his role in the 1981 firing of Paul Westhead. Whether he was right or wrong, the decision to hire Pat Riley appears to be one of the best front-office moves the Lakers ever made.

The Chapin-Prugh book was a groundbreaker in that it went well beyond the old "hits, runs, and errors" of sports reportage, describing highly intelligent UCLA basketball players questioning authority, the world around them, and long-held beliefs.

In 1968, Alcindor joined an African American boycott, organized by sociologist Harry Edwards, of the Mexico City Olympic Games. He had been expected to play for the U.S. basketball team, which won the gold medal without him, but his absence earned him mostly wrath. Alcindor also poked a hole in the bubble of West Coast racial harmony.

"In New York," he wrote in *Sports Illustrated*, "if a cat hated you, he told you to your face and you at least knew it. In California, I came across these blond guys flashing me the 'Pepsodent Beach Boy' smile to my face, then calling me a nigger behind my back."

When Alcindor was the number one draft pick of the fledgling Milwaukee Bucks in 1969, signing for the largest bonus ever paid, he seemed to have it made. USC football star O.J. Simpson was in a similar position. He represented a smiling, grateful African American athlete, the kind of guy white fans could fall in love with. Despite every gift and opportunity any man could dream of, Alcindor, on the other hand, had something negative, it seemed, to say about everything and everybody: Catholicism, white people, America, California, even the sainted John Wooden. He was dismayed to find himself in Milwaukee, perhaps the whitest city in the league. Bucks fans were underwhelmed.

Alcindor had a chance to play near his hometown. The New York Nets of the American Basketball Association made him the first pick of the ABA draft, but Milwaukee offered more money. Alcindor chose to play in the more established league. Detractors said he had no room to complain, that he was driven by money.

His first few years in the Association, Alcindor stayed away from controversy, forging the beginnings of an unparalleled career. In 1969–70 he made the All-Star team. He went up against the likes of Wilt Chamberlain in ballyhooed battles of big men. He led the Bucks from utter obscurity to the brink of the Eastern title before Willis Reed's Knicks knocked them off. The NBA's Rookie of the Year was as spectacular in his first year as Chamberlain had been.

In 1970–71, the Bucks traded for Oscar Robertson, and it made them unbeatable. Alcindor dominated play, and the Bucks smoked Los Angeles in the playoffs and then defeated Baltimore in four straight to capture the world championship. *Sports Illustrated* featured a photo of Big Lew dunking on Wes Unseld, who had in the past effectively stopped Wilt Chamberlain. They described Alcindor as doing it with such ease that he resembled a kid showing off for his mother on a playground.

However, the next three years were disappointing. In 1971, Alcindor publicly stated that he would be going by his Muslim name, Kareem Abdul-Jabbar. The name meant "noble, generous, powerful servant of God." For those who missed the announcement, a glance at the line scores was confusing, since Alcindor was nowhere to be found, but some guy named Jabbar was dominating.

He was also arrested for possession of marijuana. Shortly thereafter, Muslim revenge killings left seven people slaughtered in his Washington, D.C., town house. This all occurred after Palestinian terrorists murdered all the members of the Israeli Olympic wrestling team. His association with Islam was not viewed positively. His commitment to its tenets was questioned.

His name change also coincided with strangely confusing years in his basketball life. From 1971 to 1974, nobody even approached Abdul-Jabbar's dominance. He came after Russell had retired and Chamberlain was slowing down, never encountering a rival who could face him down as those two had done to each

With his unstoppable hook shot, the enigmatic Kareem Abdul-Jabbar was head and shoulders above his competition in the 1980s. Photo courtesy of Getty Images.

other. As an all-around player—scorer, defender, shot-blocker—there may never have been a better player than Abdul-Jabbar during this time period, yet incredibly his team failed to win the NBA title. Each playoff upset came with the sense of unbelievability, yet he walked away from those seasons without victory. Golden State's 1973 upset of the Bucks was almost impossible to comprehend.

Abdul-Jabbar perfected the most unstoppable shot in basketball history, the "skyhook." He put it up from a fairly wide arc around the basket. Because of his height and wing span nobody had a chance to deny it. All he had to do was make the shot, and he became deadly at it.

Abdul-Jabbar won three MVP awards in Milwaukee. He was generally popular in Wisconsin, albeit not at the level of a Vince

FOR THE DEFENSE

Michael Cooper was named the 1986–87 NBA Defensive Player of the Year.

Lombardi or a Paul Hornung. After a disappointing 1974–75 campaign, Abdul-Jabbar demanded a trade. He wanted to go to New York, stating that he missed the Harlem jazz scene, but was stunned to discover that he was booed in the Big Apple by the fans. They felt that his departure to UCLA had been a rejection of them.

The league desperately needed marquee players and big-market champions. To what extent the NBA directed the acquisition of Abdul-Jabbar by Los Angeles is debatable, although over the years the trading of star players to New York or L.A. has happened so often as to be predictable, not to mention rampant rumors that the draft is fixed.

Abdul-Jabbar's return to Los Angeles was a natural fit. Only a few years earlier he had been the biggest thing in L.A., literally and figuratively, his exploits well-remembered by basketball fans.

But the Lakers gave up the nucleus of their team to get Abdul-Jabbar. They were an old group that was just coming into its own after the departures of West and Chamberlain, but they were not allowed to reach fruition in order to acquire Kareem. They were also distracted by Sharman's personal problems, in the form of his wife's terminal cancer and his constant absences to be by her side.

But Kareem was brilliant even if his team was not. His 17 rebounds and 28 points per game on a bad team earned him yet another MVP award, a true rarity for a player on a losing squad. After that 40–42 year, Pete Newell stepped down as general manager. Sharman replaced him. His wife passed away and his voice was shot.

Jerry Tarkanian was almost brought in, but he was going through problems with the NCAA and wanted to "clear my name." Sharman wanted West to coach the team. West was trying to relax for the first time in his life. Without the discipline of basketball he tried to travel, play golf, and enjoy life. Instead he found himself making admittedly bad choices. Almost as if to give his life the direction he knew he needed, he accepted the Lakers job, but not without drama.

Cooke called West, but Jerry refused to return his calls. He had a lawsuit going against the owner regarding a contractual dispute in his last years. Cooke had Chick Hearn call West. Finally the lawsuit was dropped and he was hired. Coaching was not easy for him. Like all great athletes, he was frustrated at the inability of his players to perform as he had. His assistants, Stan Albeck and Jack McCloskey, often joked with him to go in for "just five minutes. Then you can retire again."

West did enjoy teaching and strategizing. He had lent himself to this part of the game as a player his whole career, but he disliked the organizational details that go with coaching. He also found the nervousness that he had used to fuel his clutch play to be a hindrance in communication with players when the game was on the line.

Julius Erving was made available when the ABA broke up, and West told Cooke to go after him. Cooke refused to spend the kind of money "Dr. J" was on the market for. Free agency in sports was quickly getting out of hand. Few had a handle on how to deal with it. The old West-Cooke feud heated up again. Cooke claimed that West's claims were "balderdash" and that West used the failure to get Erving as an excuse for the "dreadful" job he did as coach.

"That blows my mind, knowing they turned down Dr. J.," Kareem said. "Mr. Cooke screwed up royally on that one. You do what you can do to improve your team."

The Philadelphia 76ers, who signed Dr. J, spent twice on payroll what the Lakers of that era were spending, without the resources. Despite West's problems with Cooke, he was an effective coach. Not having ever coached at any level, he admitted his inexperience, but Kareem admired his up-front approach. He said West "does something to bring you near the top of your skills."

According to Kareem, it was only last-month injuries to Kermit Washington and Lucius Allen that prevented the 1976–77

Lakers, who vaulted to the best regular-season record (53–29) in the NBA, from going all the way. Instead, Bill Walton and Portland swept them four straight en route to the title. It was a snapshot of what might have been.

Walton had followed Alcindor as the next great UCLA center. From 1971 to 1974, he led the Bruins to two NCAA titles and the completion of their 88-game winning streak. Walton, also a three-time national Player of the Year, looked to be every bit as dominant as Alcindor. In his senior year, however, the team got complacent and lost four games, including a Final Four overtime heartbreaker to David "Skywalker" Thompson and North Carolina State.

Walton entered the NBA amid great fanfare. After a slow start he came into his own in 1977. For two years he was the most over-powering player in the game, but he had always been injury prone—knees, feet, joints, bones, bizarre maladies—and his promising career never reached the heights Kareem attained.

But had Walton been at his best over a decade's period of time, theirs would have been a rivalry to match Russell-Chamberlain or Larry Bird versus Magic Johnson. Even in 1977, the year Walton and Portland took the NBA title, his injuries kept him from capturing the MVP award that went to Kareem (26 points with 13 rebounds a game).

Abdul-Jabbar bristled at the notion that he was outplayed by the white Walton and that people had the temerity to possess knowledge of it. The reporters at the *L.A. Herald-Examiner* in particular "were killing him," according to West, adding that the two writers, Rich Levin and Ted Green, should have been fired. But West contributed. Frustrated over losses, he opened his mouth in

FIGHTING MAD

Shaquille O'Neal gets fouled so much that there is a name for it: "Hack-a-Shaq."

public when he should have stayed quiet, one time calling Kareem "a dog," and later admitting he was not cut out for coaching.

The late 1970s were "wilderness years" for Abdul-Jabbar and the Lakers, but in 1979 the drafting of Magic Johnson began their greatest run. He and the 33-year-old Abdul-Jabbar spurred L.A. to a 60-win season and the NBA title over Erving's Sixers.

"I know the game a lot better," Abdul-Jabbar said at that time. "I'm physically stronger…and I'm still quicker than most centers in the league."

In 1979–80, he earned his sixth Most Valuable Player award. In the 1980s the Lakers captured five championships and nine division crowns. The Magic-Kareem duo was perfect, with Kareem scoring 20 points a game well into his thirties but ceding much of the responsibility on offense to floor-leader Magic.

As retirement neared, Abdul-Jabbar mellowed, developing a friendlier relationship with fans and media. His natural intelligence and gentle nature overcame his early taciturn ways. His "farewell tour" of the league after announcing his retirement in 1988–89 was one of the best sendoffs in basketball history. Best of all, Kareem learned how to laugh at himself. The farewell tour allowed for many lighthearted moments.

In 1984 Abdul-Jabbar scored his 31,420[th] point to pass Chamberlain as the league's all-time scorer. The Lakers teams of the 1985–88 period under coach Pat Riley are among the greatest in pro basketball history. In 1985 it appeared that Boston's Robert Parish stopped Kareem, but Kareem proved the critics wrong by leading L.A. to victory against a great defending-champion Celtics team.

"What you saw was passion," Riley told the media.

"The '80s made up for all the abuses I took during the '70s," he told a reporter after retirement. "I outlived all my critics. By the time I retired, everybody saw me as a venerable institution. Things do change."

After finishing with 38,387 points (a 24.6 career average) and six titles, Abdul-Jabbar was elected to the Hall of Fame.

"I think I played basically for an idea, which is how close I could come to being at my best," he said. "I put some hard work

THE GOOD, THE BAD, AND THE UGLY

The question was: who is the most important Laker—Shaq O'Neal, Kobe Bryant, or Phil Jackson? Shaq left after the 2003–04 season. Jackson did, too, but returned. Kobe stuck around. Events surrounding the Lakers have ranged from the good, the bad, and the ugly. Shaq led the 2005–06 Miami Heat to the NBA title.

into that, I had the good fortune to have been given talent, and I was lucky enough not to have gotten hurt...

"I always knew this would have to end.... People find new heroes."

He decided to go into coaching, but this created controversy again when he did not get hired. He brought up racism and other bogus issues as the reason. But he did show a passion for teaching and after a number of years coaching on an Indian reservation came back to the NBA with the Clippers. Eventually Phil Jackson and the Lakers brought him on as a special assistant.

BASKETBALL ROYALTY

Earvin "Magic" Johnson was basketball royalty in a city that reveres the game. He was made for the Lakers, a team that was perfect for Los Angeles. It is difficult to imagine him playing any-place else. Imagine if Larry Bird had been a Laker and Johnson a Celtic. Ted Williams was once almost traded for Joe DiMaggio, but in the end it seemed unthinkable. The same thing with Magic.

He grew up in East Lansing, Michigan. His mother was very religious, so much so that when her son was given the nickname Magic, she objected that it had occult overtones. It was at Everett High School in East Lansing where Earvin transformed into "Magic." A local sportswriter named Fred Stanley gave him the name. He was tall enough to handle the center position, but he did it all. He could dribble, pass, shoot, rebound, block. He was the complete package, but better yet, from the very beginning his greatest attribute was a knack for team play.

Winnin' time.

For Magic, the choice of a college was fairly easy. Michigan State University was located right there in East Lansing, where his mother, family, and friends—and he had a lot already—could watch him play for the Spartans.

Big Ten basketball was pretty good, but not at the level of the Pac-8 conference, which of course meant UCLA, but over the years it had produced national champions at Oregon State, Stanford, and California. In 1971 UCLA had finished number one in the nation, USC number two.

Ohio State had been the class of the Big Ten, winning the 1960 national title. Michigan was strong, making it to the 1965 NCAA title game before UCLA blew them away. But the conference was seen as more physical than athletic. In many ways they suffered from the same comparison as in football, where their teams played a "three yards and a cloud of dust" offensive style, always losing to the Pac 8 in Rose Bowls.

Because of integration, population shifts, and good weather, the West Coast was still the dominant region for collegiate sports in the 1970s. San Francisco had been a national basketball power and briefly flirted with that again in the mid-1970s. The Southeastern and Atlantic Coast conferences were not as dominant as they are today. The great baseball players, track stars, tennis players, Olympians—they always seemed to be from California.

But in 1975 there was a hint of change in the Big Ten, when a young former Buckeye sixth man came over from Army, where he had coached the cadets' basketball team. Bobby Knight led Indiana to an unbeaten season going into the Final Four. The expected battle between Knight and UCLA's John Wooden did not occur when the Hoosiers lost to Kentucky. UCLA won their last national title (until 1995) by upending the Wildcats, which was even more symbolic. Wooden had built UCLA into a powerhouse by recruiting blacks. Kentucky had lost panache because they did not.

The next year IU came back, went undefeated, and this time took it all the way to the NCAA title. By the time Magic Johnson was a high school senior in 1977, the Big Ten was gaining prestige in basketball. Whereby a few years earlier a blue chipper like Magic would have been mesmerized by John Wooden and the promise of L.A.'s bright lights, now Spartans coach Jud Heathcote was able to keep this particular homegrown talent at home.

"I'm asked a lot what was the greatest thing Earvin did," Heathcote said. "Many would say passing the ball, his great court sense, the fact that he could rebound. I say the greatest things Earvin did were intangible. He always made guys he played with better. In summer pickup games, Earvin would take three or four nonplayers, and he'd make those guys look so much better, and they would win, not because he was making the baskets all by himself, but because he just made other players better."

"You're running down the floor and you're open and most people can't get the ball to you through two or three people, but all of a sudden the ball's in your hands and you've got a layup," said Terry Donnelly, Magic's teammate and roommate at Michigan State.

Heathcote deserves recognition for seeing Johnson's back-court skills. When he first put the 6'9" high school center at guard people thought he was crazy, and at first there were growing pains. But the coach recognized the enormous advantage of having Johnson mobilized instead of fixed at the low corner. He could pass over people on the press. His height gave him tremendous advantage in spotting and angling passes to open men anywhere on the court.

His speed, agility, and athleticism allowed him to hit the boards and score. Heathcote helped turn Magic from a very good player into a once-in-a-lifetime star. Had he not been made into a guard in college, the Lakers never would have done it. When Magic got to the pros he was moved to forward, but Heathcote said they should move him from forward to guard, and after some experimentation that is what happened.

"Actually, he was very comfortable in all those areas," said Heathcote. "When he went to the pros and right away they had him playing forward, I said sooner or later they'll realize that Earvin can play anywhere on defense and he has to have the ball on offense."

Exhibit A: Game 6 versus Philadelphia, 1980.

Johnson's performance in leading Michigan State to the 1979 NCAA title has been well chronicled. He outplayed Larry Bird of Indiana State in front of a huge TV audience. Neither "March Madness" nor pro basketball has been the same since. In his rookie year Kareem needed rebounding help, so Magic filled in at power forward on the defensive end. But Norm Nixon could not handle the entire backcourt workload, so Magic was brought alongside him, too. Eventually, Nixon was moved to shooting guard, Magic to point.

But Magic's greatest contribution was in his attitude. It was the fall of 1979, and the team was in their "morass" period. Attendance, TV ratings, and inspiration were all down. The players were considered drug users and womanizers. Fans were bored. The big-market teams were off, and the nation found little enthusiasm for Seattle, Washington, and Portland.

Kareem Abdul-Jabbar seemed to be going through the motions. The team was heading nowhere. Magic Johnson added

THINGS TO SAVOR

Jerry Buss loved the world-renowned USC Song Girls who danced on the sidelines of his alma mater's football and basketball games. When he took over the Lakers, he brought together former song leaders from SC and also UCLA, forming the original Laker Girls.

Today, they are considered the "gold standard" of professional basketball cheerleaders. Their dance moves are unique and have spawned numerous music videos. They have danced in Asia, Europe, and Australia. The Laker Girls have performed before U.S. troops in Italy, Bosnia, Korea, Japan, Israel, and Sarajevo. Naturally, being in Los Angeles, becoming a Laker Girl often leads to opportunities in the greater entertainment industry. The most famous of the Laker Girls is pop star Paula Abdul.

five years or more to his career. After losing to Seattle in the 1979 playoffs, the L.A. media fixed on Kareem. He had been in Los Angeles four years and not produced a champion. His place in the game's history was in question—a superstar, but a disappointing one.

"At that time Kareem seemed to be going through a peculiar questioning in his life," said former *L.A. Times* sports reporter Ted Green. "He seemed to be wondering if he wanted to continue playing basketball. He was often lethargic and apathetic on the floor. Many nights he operated on cruise control. One night in Madison Square Garden he scored 24 points and had only one rebound. I wrote a story and called him Abdul-Sleepwalker. He got very upset and didn't speak to me for several months."

Abdul-Jabbar does not buy the theory that he was energized by Magic's presence, but whatever happened, it was a great thing for all concerned, regardless of where the credit lies.

Johnson embraced his teammates, inviting them to his house for lunch. The future was clearly laid out in the very first game of his pro career. Kareem's skyhook at the buzzer won the opener at San Diego. Magic gave Kareem a giant hug, celebrating as if they had just won the title. Kareem was taken aback but slightly amused. He told Magic they had 81 more to go.

From 1982 to 1987, Magic's scoring average increased consistently. He also led the league in assists each of those years except one. Johnson's low point came in 1984. Fans and media said Bird had passed him as the greater of the two players, even though Magic still possessed two NBA titles to Larry's one, in addition to having beaten Bird in the 1979 NCAA championship game. Some disparaged him, calling him "Tragic" Johnson.

Magic earned three MVP awards, his first coming in 1987. With Abdul-Jabbar sidelined part of the season with an eye infection, Magic responded by scoring almost 24 points per game (his career high). He won his third Finals Most Valuable Player award that year. He won the 1989 and 1990 NBA MVP award in years in which the team did not capture the championship. On April 15, 1991, Johnson passed Oscar Robertson as the all-time assist leader with 9,888.

After a high-profile college career at Michigan State and a memorable college championship victory over Larry Bird, Magic Johnson did things with the ball people had never seen before and electrified Los Angeles upon his arrival.

THEN CAME SHAQ

In many ways, Shaquille O'Neal represents, especially to Lakers fans, the hopes and dreams of Wilt Chamberlain. Chamberlain was a larger-than-life figure whose expectations were just as large. He was no failure, having won the 1967 NBA championship in Philadelphia and the 1972 banner in L.A., but considering his talents, there could have been so much more.

Symbolically, Wilt passed away in 1999, the year Shaq started his team on the road to three straight NBA championships. Even larger than Wilt (7'1", 330 pounds), he dominated even more, at least in their respective L.A. years. Shaq left no doubt.

O'Neal's stepfather was an army sergeant. While O'Neal's size and athletic skills are extraordinary, there is little doubt that the mental discipline he got from being the stepson of a military man played as big a role in his success as any other factor. It was not always easy. Young Shaq grew up in New Jersey, Germany, Georgia, and Texas.

When Shaq was a youngster living on an army base in Fulda, Germany, he got into trouble. His stepfather directed him to a basketball clinic in which Louisiana State University coach Dale Brown was the visiting speaker. The 6'6" junior high school student made a big impression on the coach. Brown stayed in close contact with him throughout his extraordinary career at Cole High School in Texas. In 1989 he was the most recruited player in the nation. But the Brown connection stuck, and he became an LSU Tiger.

O'Neal dominated collegiate basketball in 1991 and 1992, becoming the top pick of the Orlando Magic. From 1992 to 1999, O'Neal was one of the best players in the NBA, but his teams met with frustration in the playoffs. Michael Jordan's Bulls dominated the decade. As Jordan reached retirement, O'Neal was seen as the marquee name in the league.

In 1994, Shaq performed as a basketball player very similar to himself in William Friedkin's *Blue Chips*, a revealing look at the corrupting influences of money in big-time collegiate basketball. He was excellent, flashing a charismatic smile and likable quality that led him to movies and music as hobbies. Shaq always demonstrated intelligence and wisdom beyond his years, no doubt the effect of his sergeant stepdad.

His "Hollywood side" made him a natural for Los Angeles, where he signed as a free agent for $121 million prior to the 1996–97 season. But from 1996 to 1999, Shaq's Lakers were not successful in the playoffs. There were injuries, arguments with teenage star Kobe Bryant, dissension, and disagreements with coaches.

But 1999 was the year everything started to come together. Bryant matured as a player and as a man. STAPLES Center opened for business. Phil Jackson came in as coach. Los Angeles won their first world championship in 12 years.

In 1999–2000 the Lakers won 67 games, with O'Neal leading the way (first in the NBA with 29.7 points, a .574 shooting percentage, plus three blocks and 13.6 rebounds a game). He was the Most Valuable Player in the league.

"Prior to last year I thought he was just a dunker," said John Wooden, an astute observer of the L.A. basketball scene. "But this year his court vision got better, he shared the ball willingly, and I

All eyes were on Shaq when he joined the Lakers, and he was determined to dominate upon his arrival in 1996.

thought he showed more moves around the basket, so I'd have to say he's more of a complete player than ever before."

In the 2000 playoffs, Los Angeles beat Sacramento in five, Phoenix in five, and Portland in seven games. In averaging 38 points and almost 17 rebounds, O'Neal took home the Finals MVP trophy along with the world championship after a six-game win over Indiana. It ended a long cold spell in Los Angeles. In the entire decade of the 1990s, the only championship had been UCLA's basketball title of 1995.

"No man can stop him, and you can't play a zone, so I guess they figure with enough big bodies they'll wear him down, but Shaquille loves a challenge, so it'll be interesting," said Tex Winter, Phil Jackson's invaluable assistant.

In 2000–01, O'Neal scored 29 points a game during the regular season and then led the Lakers to a postseason record of 11 consecutive wins to start the playoffs. In sweeping past the Trail Blazers, Kings, and Spurs before taking the 76ers in five games to finish with a 15–1 postseason mark, O'Neal was the Finals MVP.

History was made the next year when Los Angeles earned its third straight title. Shaq again led the way with 27 points a game. L.A. broke the record by winning 12 straight road playoff games. The Finals saw the outgunned New Jersey Nets falling in four straight.

While Shaq's three-year run was impressive for him and the team, there was a sense that the rivalries of old—Wilt and Russell, Celtics and Lakers, Magic and Bird—were more exciting. It was almost too easy, especially for old-time Lakers fans who had suffered through so much disappointment. Similarly, as great as Michael Jordan was in Chicago, his accomplishments did not seem to have been won over worthy opponents in quite the same manner as those of Wilt, Russell, West, Magic, and Bird. Some complained that free agency caused occasional monopolies. Neither O'Neal nor Jordan seemed to have had played in a league with anybody nearly as good as they were in their prime.

In addition to his pro exploits, O'Neal won a gold medal at Atlanta as a member of "Dream Team II," and he earned his degree from LSU in 2000.

WINNERS AND WHINERS

1968-69: SOAP OPERA

In May of 1968, Philadelphia 76ers owner Irving Kosloff phoned Jack Kent Cooke at his Forum office.

"Would the Lakers be interested in Wilt Chamberlain?" asked Kosloff.

Cooke was not quite sure what he had heard, but he had heard it. He had to struggle just to reply in measured tones, and he said simply, "We certainly would be."

Chamberlain wanted out of Philadelphia. The times, they were a-changin'. Chamberlain, a single guy, certainly had his eye on the ladies in Southern California. The old days, when an African American man had to stay on a straight and narrow course in order to avoid white scrutiny, was becoming a thing of the past, especially out in California, home of the free speech movement, the antiwar movement, and the "Summer of Love."

Chamberlain envisioned getting enough of Jack Kent Cooke's dollars to buy one of those movie star mansions in the hills and to live that very lifestyle. He wanted to be in L.A. year-round, to avoid the bitter East Coast winters and hone his beach volleyball skills.

His desire to be a Laker had a melodramatic quality to it, too. Jerry West, Elgin Baylor, and the team were as frustrated about being on the losing end of their rivalry with Russell and the Celtics as Chamberlain had been, so why would he want to join an outfit that had not been able to defeat the hated Bostons?

SOCIAL PROGRESS

Wilt Chamberlain was the first man of color to represent a full line of clothing (LeTigre's Big and Tall).

On the other hand, Wilt had overcome Boston in 1967, which was one time more than West, Baylor, & Co. up to that time. But the bottom line was that Chamberlain observed the Lakers and figured that if he became one of them, they would be unbeatable.

"We'll simply have the best team in basketball history," said the man who just one year earlier had been a member of the team thought to be, up to then, the best ever.

In June 1968 Wilt Chamberlain visited Jack Kent Cooke at his Bel Air mansion. That experience alone shaped him. He wanted to live in that neighborhood, which sits on a hill above the UCLA campus, adjacent to Westwood, the exclusive enclave of Brentwood just on the other side of the San Diego Freeway. Sunset Boulevard winds around down below to the Holmby Hills neighborhood where Hugh Hefner's mansion is, and beyond that into Beverly Hills, then the famed Sunset Strip where no doubt Chamberlain envisioned himself being the "king of L.A.," surrounded by young lovelies and admiring sycophants in a phalanx of celebrityhood.

From the exclusive canyons and vistas of Bel Air, where Cooke's neighbors included Charlton Heston and Jack Nicholson, the view stretched itself out in scenic, regal splendor: the mid-Wilshire, downtown, the hills stretching into the San Gabriel Mountains to the east; the Santa Monica range to the west; the endless strand of beaches; the Palos Verdes Peninsula; on a clear day, Catalina Island; Orange County out in the distance.

A man could look out upon this and dream big dreams, which was Wilt Chamberlain's style. Wilt was already wealthy by pro sports standards, but he wanted to be wealthy as in "old money" wealthy. The very man who could help him achieve that goal had invited him to his home for the express purpose of helping him do just that! In California, the land of the gold rush and Hollywood, "old money" was your latest bank deposit.

Wilt noted that they both drove a 1962 Bentley. Cooke, by no means a racist and certainly a man who by this point must have been comfortable with African American people, was still probably knocked flat by Wilt's intelligence and breadth of knowledge. Here was this giant man from the Philadelphia projects who was held up as a symbol of brutal physicality, yet he carried on an erudite discussion with the owner about antique furniture, art, and the intricacies of the English language.

Chamberlain had educated opinions about the Vietnam War, the upcoming 1968 presidential campaign (one of America's all-time humdingers, affected greatly by the assassination of Robert F. Kennedy, within a few days of their meeting and a few miles from Cooke's mansion in the Ambassador Hotel on Wilshire Boulevard). It was very likely Chamberlain's personality and an immediate symbiosis with Cooke that resulted in Wilt's becoming the highest-paid pro athlete of all time after that day: five years, $1,250,000, $250,000 per season.

A trade needed to be consummated. The 76ers virtually handed one of the greatest players in the game's storied history to Los Angeles for the journeyman Darrall Imhoff and two others, Archie Clark and Jerry Chambers. They immediately became terrible, and a few years later made it official: in 1973 they had the worst record in NBA history.

The problems with Wilt? Philadelphia is a funny city: a dirty, gritty, hard-core town with hard-core fans. A great big, outspoken black man who loved women—white women, at that—was controversial enough. But they still clung to the belief that he was a selfish player who could not beat Russell. He did it once, but when the old master came back the next year to knock Wilt off his mountaintop it seemed to Wilt and the Sixers time to depart. What better place to reinvent oneself than in another division in the land of dreams?

In L.A. it looked great, but a lot of old-school basketball types saw something inherently wrong. The "trade" was more an act of free agency, the money outrageous. Cooke was trying to build "the best team money can buy" in a game where purists thought success came from the draft, the careful nurturing of young talent into veteran success.

The question of whether a bunch of guys who collectively had lost to Bill Russell more than 10 times could beat Bill Russell was intriguing. But the biggest hullabaloo came over the question of scoring and ego.

Baylor and West were already scoring machines—one white, one African American. They respected each other, but many suspected each wanted to get more chances to put the ball in the hoop. Now, a third scoring machine—the greatest ever—was going to encroach on their shot opportunities.

"I wonder if Jerry West and Elgin Baylor are going to be willing to be underlings to Wilt Chamberlain?" mocked Celtics general manager Red Auerbach.

Chamberlain was defensive about the premise, Cooke infuriated.

"A statement like that is typical of Mr. Genius," slammed Cooke. "It's preposterous."

Apparently, however, Cooke had conducted the entire deal—trade and negotiations—without directly consulting Butch van Breda Kolff. Van Breda Kolff was at a party in Santa Barbara when he heard about it.

"He was upset by the trade," said Bill Bertka. "Butch didn't have anything against Chamberlain or his effectiveness. But you had to have Chamberlain in the post, and that dictated a style of offense that Butch didn't particularly like. He'd rather have all five men moving, all five men interchangeable and sharing the ball."

Then the press got into it. Van Breda Kolff told the media he could "handle" Chamberlain. Chamberlain did not think he needed "handling." When the two men met at a charity function in New York City that summer, an argument ensued in which Chamberlain refused to pose for a photo with his new coach.

The soap opera was now in full swing.

This of course carried over into training camp, which started shortly thereafter. Chamberlain, in van Breda Kolff's eyes, hustled the first day but slacked off after that. Chamberlain, the guy who would have signed with the NBA out of high school if he could have, who left KU a year early when that was unheard of, was unimpressed by the "college" methods of a guy just a few years removed from not just a collegiate program but an Ivy League program at that. In Wilt's mind, he was playing for Cooke, who had traded for him, had negotiated with him, and had respect for him. Van Breda Kolff was an obstacle to Chamberlain's vision of himself: a "partner" of Cooke's, almost a part owner (although the owner would have raised an eyebrow over that concept), a guy invested in the team in a way that no athlete before him ever had been. He was a groundbreaker, he knew it, and that was that. Chamberlain was indeed a guy who, by virtue of his race, his size, his enormous salary, and his effect on everything around him, symbolized an entirely new kind of athlete.

Baseball star Reggie Jackson—similar to Chamberlain in terms of race, intellect, pride, and ability—saw Chamberlain as a template. Jackson's attitude about salary and the resulting battles over money with controversial owner Charlie O. Finley would be fought publicly and with much bloodshed, but eventually Reggie would become a Chamberlain-like figure. He would become rich enough and large enough to include himself in discussions over team ownership. Over time, the concept of the player as a part owner would become possible—rare, but not out of the realm.

But Chamberlain's situation was different from Reggie's. Reggie and his teammates united in common dislike of Finley. Chamberlain's problems were with his coach, the guy he and his new teammates needed to be on the same page with every day.

HALL OF THE VERY GOOD

Mel Counts was a Laker from 1966 to 1970 and again from 1972 to 1974. A seven-footer from Oregon State, he was almost as physically imposing as Wilt Chamberlain. He averaged 9.7 points scoring for the Lakers.

Not surprisingly, the rift caused problems on the court. Naturally, the season opener featured Wilt versus his old club, the 76ers, and in a game in which Chamberlain suddenly seemed unwilling to score, the Sixers beat Los Angeles.

In the next game, Chamberlain changed tactics, scoring big in a victory over New York. In the fifth game, he was outrebounded by Wes Unseld of the Bullets. The season had barely begun, but already Chamberlain and his coach were communicating through the media, which is never a good sign.

Van Breda Kolff benched Wilt, to the chagrin of Cooke. It was a great big tabloid story that the media, especially in sensationalist L.A., ate up with a fork and spoon.

"There are deficiencies with every club," Chamberlain told the assorted media. "Here with the Lakers, I've tried to blend in, lend myself to the deficiencies, try to help overcome them. Here with the likes of Jerry and Elgin we have people who can score. So I've simply tried to get the rebounds, get the ball to one of them so we can score."

Questions about Chamberlain's huge salary overshadowed his play, but the team was drawing at home, on the road, and on television. Color TV was now all the rage. The Lakers seemed made for it with their gold uniforms outlayed against "Forum blue," the camera panning the crowd for shots of actresses and celebrities. Chamberlain was *worth* what Cooke was paying him, and that was an obvious, bottom-line fact.

At home, Chamberlain was cheered. Fans judged the situation. They saw the 7'1" superstar dishing off to West and Baylor, selflessly trying to help the team win, and were won over to his side. He was cheered lustily at home. This was an entirely new dynamic.

BUSINESS COMES FIRST

The acquisition of Wilt Chamberlain in 1968 was similar to the acquisition of Shaquille O'Neal almost three decades later. Championships did not immediately occur, but ultimate glory eventually did.

Philadelphia fans have a notorious reputation for being "boo birds." Their treatment of Chamberlain was as much a reason for this as any. Whether race had anything to do with it or not, despite his gargantuan feats, Chamberlain was never a beloved figure in his hometown. L.A., on the other hand, received him with open arms.

When all else is said and done, however, a team's performance, based on its wins and losses, is the final arbiter of success. In this respect, as the regular season played out, the experiment appeared to work. Not unexpectedly, it took a while. Van Breda Kolff was a proponent of an offensive scheme not unlike the triangle offense that was started at USC in the 1940s and made popular by Phil Jackson and Tex Winter with the Bulls and Lakers.

But the triangle was not designed around a pure post scorer like Chamberlain, even if he dished out half the time. Wilt was not a guy who was going to run around, spending time at the top of the key. But his presence under the basket sometimes blocked Baylor's drives to the left low post. With his injury, Baylor was no longer as effective with this maneuver, but van Breda Kolff insisted on moving Wilt to the high post to make room for Elgin. Of course this reduced Wilt's rebounding numbers.

There were shouting matches. Fred Schaus was brought in as a peacemaker, but of course he had no history with Wilt, who began to see conspiracies around every corner. The coach and the center agreed to stop bad-mouthing each other in the press. Then the players had a meeting, airing their problems with Wilt's on-court demeanor. He was asked to spend time with his teammates away from the arena, a reference to his entourage, his women, and the attendant circus that was his life.

Certainly if Wilt slept with twenty thousand women, averaging 1.2 per day beginning at age 15, these were the days when he was, uh, padding his statistics. For a while normalcy prevailed, but a February 3 loss to Seattle led to a screaming match between player and coach. Chamberlain thought West and Baylor—West in particular—were favored over him. Baylor had to prevent an actual fight, which says something since Chamberlain despised fighting. They screamed "like animals."

After that, Chamberlain submitted, asking van Breda Kolff what he wanted of him. He was told to simply play defense and rebound. Finally, the club jelled and rolled to a 55–27 mark, good for first place in the Western Division. They were the class of the NBA, an odds-on favorite to win the championship.

With Chamberlain dominating underneath, L.A. gave up only 108 points a game, fourth best in the league. Wilt averaged 21.1 rebounds (a club record to this day) and 20.5 points per game (.583 shooting). On March 11 versus Detroit, Wilt converted a perfect 14-of-14 from the floor. Baylor scored 24.8 a game and West 25.9 a game. Keith Erickson, another ex-Bruin, played a key role.

Unlike past years, in which the NBA was competitive, with several teams challenging Boston for supremacy, the league looked weak when the 1969 playoffs started. Nobody could stop Los Angeles in the West. The Sixers were not a factor anymore. Boston was old, old, old. Russell looked creaky, his cast of veteran teammates a shell of their old selves. It seemed to be a joke that they qualified for the playoffs with a losing record, but in the "second season" they got hot and advanced to the Finals.

Based upon their regular-season records, it seemed impossible that Boston could beat the Lakers this time. L.A.'s day had arrived. In each of the previous Finals losses to Boston, Jerry West acknowledged that they had the better team, but in 1969 his patience ran out. It was too much for him to bear.

"We were better," said West. "Period. And we didn't win. And that was the toughest one."

In the last regular-season meeting between the two teams, Los Angeles destroyed a limping, gimping Russell- and Sam Jones–led Celtics, 108–73, on national television. With home-court advantage, L.A. was confident, but beneath the hubris was a concern that Baylor was so worn out that he had nothing left for the postseason.

Game 1 was an eye-opener. The team that had lost 108–73 forced West to single-handedly score 53 points in a two-point Lakers win that Russell called "the greatest clutch performance ever against the Celtics."

"I GOT YOU, BABE."

Photos of Pat Riley when he was with the San Diego Rockets reveal an absolute Sonny Bono look-alike.

The dynamics of the matchups had changed with Chamberlain's presence, but West was exhausted after the game. Despite victory, there was a sense of foreboding—that such heroics were still necessary if the team was to prevail over a club that, by all rights, they should be able to beat in five or six.

Enter John Havlicek, Boston's "Mr. Clutch." Unlike his teammates, "Hondo" (his real nickname, after a John Wayne movie) was not tired. He raced up and down the court, scoring 43 to West's 41. Russell held Chamberlain to an unheard-of four points, but he rebounded well. But Baylor scored the team's last 12 points, and after the 118–112 Lakers win their 2–0 series lead looked impregnable.

Smelly old Boston Garden reminded them that a series sweep was not in the cards. The Celtics went up early, but L.A. roared back and seemed ready to take an insurmountable 3–0 lead in the fourth quarter. Havlicek, one eye shut after getting poked by Erickson's finger, hit clutch free throws to secure a six-point Boston win. It was a psychological blow to Los Angeles, but the events of Game 4 destroyed their fragile sense of superiority.

West, a Christian man, had to find solace in "the Lord's will" in order to make sense of the 89–88 loss. Russell outcoached van Breda Kolff, and his team put all their effort into defense, which worked. Both teams were forced into sloppy offensive play. Nobody could score, but Los Angeles led by one point with 15 seconds to go and had possession of the ball.

Key steals in these situations mark the Celtics legend, and so it was on this occasion, leading to an agonizing last possession in which Sam Jones missed the jumper but Boston wrested the rebound away from L.A. They desperately tried to set picks for a final shot, but Jones was forced into an off-balance heave from 18 feet out that had no chance.

Chamberlain had to pull his hand away to avoid goaltending. The ball clanked on the rim, bounced high on the top of the backboard, and descended down. Wilt faced the basket, still unable to snatch it lest he be called for goaltending. He watched in anguish as it dropped straight through the net, giving Boston the win and a 2–2 tie.

Jones fed the writers a load about arc, backspin, and the like, causing teammate Larry Siegfried to laugh and state that the Hall of Famer was "entitled" at this point to "blow a little smoke."

It was typical "Celtic luck," infuriating to the Lakers. The rivalry now was taking on the same kind of ethnic and cultural passions as the famed Notre Dame–Southern California football tradition, without the trade-off in victories that have marked the Irish and Trojans over the decades.

It would have been too convenient, of course, for Los Angeles to implode then and there, to return home, fold in front of the home fans, and begin the summer of their discontent. Instead, Chamberlain had one of the greatest rebounding games of his career, holding Russell to a bucket; West poured in 39, and with the 117–104 win L.A. could taste it.

Game 6 was tough to swallow. As if by fate, Jerry had injured his hamstring in his 39-point Game 5 effort, slowing him considerably when his team needed him in the wake of Chamberlain's failure to show up and play, scoring only two points. Boston 99, Los Angeles 90.

Game 7: with West's hammie wrapped, he hobbled onto the floor and looked up at the Forum rafters. There, to his horror, were thousands of balloons waiting to be released. Cooke, assuming victory, ordered Forum employees to spend hours blowing up and setting in place balloons, which he planned to unleash to the tune

"WELL, THERE YOU GO AGAIN."

After the Lakers won the 1985 NBA title, they visited President Ronald Reagan at the White House.

of "Happy Days Are Here Again" as soon Los Angeles earned the victory. Auerbach and Russell saw the balloons and used them as motivation to fire up their team for one final try before Bill's retirement at season's end. The Celtics dynasty, at least the legendary one that had dominated NBA play since the 1950s, was over but for that one last game. A new generation would have to emerge, but it would be several years down the road.

Cooke's memo to the Forum staff, outlining the precise plans for the victory celebration, was passed around the Celtics locker room to various guffaws and reactions of steely determination. West heard about it and knew that all was lost. In the game of inches that is professional sports at the highest level—and Lakers-Celtics is pro sports at its highest level—West knew that the margin for error was too narrow to overcome the psychological edge that Boston gained in the face of Lakers overconfidence. West was disgusted that it was not he or his teammates who were giving this bulletin-board edge to Boston, but rather the Canadian Caesar-owner, who probably would have marched the Celtics through the streets of downtown L.A. like prisoners from Gaul after the win had he been allowed to.

It would not come to pass. The Celtics were on fire early and held off subsequent Lakers efforts at getting back into the game, going into the half with a three-point lead. It was not the lead, three points being a small margin, but rather the tides and swings of the game, which an experienced observer of sports or politics can detect and use to predict the final outcome, which made the result obvious.

Los Angeles fought back but expended themselves with each effort. West was brilliant but bandaged, a figure out of Greek tragedy trying to keep the Lakers ship from succumbing to the siren song of defeat. Instead, the ship continued perilously close to shore until it crashed into the rocks.

Boston led 71–62 with five minutes to go in the third quarter. West scored, but Russell replied with a score that drew Chamberlain's fifth foul. For 885 NBA games Chamberlain had never fouled out, but now one of his greatest advantages—the ability to play freely without fear of leaving the game on fouls—

was lost to him. Van Breda Kolff left him in, Russell went aggressive, and the tentative Chamberlain was unable to stop him. Boston went up 91–76 going into the fourth quarter, and the Forum sounded like a church.

But Russell and Jones were exhausted. Havlicek and Jones got in foul trouble. Chamberlain injured his knee and asked to be taken out. With Wilt on the bench, it seemed to free Los Angeles up to play with abandon, a style West was good at. "Mr. Clutch" made a series of shots and free throws, heroically pulling the Lakers back to within nine with 5:45 to go, then three, then after a Mel Counts jumper with three minutes left, one point (103–102).

At this point the moment that defined the entire soap opera season of 1968–69 occurred. Chamberlain asked to go back in. Van Breda Kolff, perhaps impressed by Counts's play and clutch shot, perhaps wanting the free-flowing style to continue, perhaps concerned that Chamberlain would foul out, for whatever reason informed the big man that the team was doing well enough without him and to sit down. It was not quite saying, "We don't need you," but it was close.

Cooke did not realize it, thinking Chamberlain was injured and unable to come back. West thought the same thing. West later expressed that it was perhaps the worst decision of any Lakers coach. Cooke's later actions spoke louder than words.

In the Shakespearean way of thinking that surrounded these Lakers, however, it was all part of the script. West knocked the ball away, Don Nelson grabbed it and threw up a prayer. It did the same thing Jones's "backspin arc" shot in Game 4 had done—clanking off the rim, bouncing high in the air, then dropping through the net as if guided by an unseen spirit, the kind wearing a green tam-o'-shanter.

Chamberlain sat and watched. The Lakers missed a couple and the Celtics committed an offensive foul. Buckets were traded off. Time withered away, Boston holding on by the barest of margins, 108–106. It was their 11th NBA championship. The Lakers had not won one since moving to the West Coast.

West immediately had to use all his common sense to remind himself that he had his health, his faith, his family. Otherwise,

Despite their apparent athletic superiority, Wilt Chamberlain and the Lakers were frustrated by Bill Russell and the Celtics in the 1969 Finals.

his anger and disappointment would have been almost too much to bear.

The soap opera reached epic proportions in the aftermath, with recriminations abounding in subsequent editions of the *Los Angeles Times*. The press quickly discovered that Wilt's injury was not as serious as they had assumed and that "Big Norman" had asked to be put back in the game with five minutes to go.

Cooke was infuriated, West incredulous. Bill Russell, about to retire, was free to offer his opinion, which was that Chamberlain had for all practical purposes quit, letting his team down by not playing. He probably was unaware at the time that the coach had kept him out, but the remarks ended a friendship he shared with Wilt that was not repaired for years. Others said the "friendship" was manufactured by Russell, playing psychology with Wilt. It was felt that Russell had kept Wilt down by feigning good feelings instead of awakening the "sleeping giant."

Havlicek told him, "I love you." Boston spared nothing in honoring the fallen hero, but the classy West was disconsolate, further tortured by the fact that the car he won for being the only Most Valuable Player from a losing team was *green*.

The balloons were painstakingly removed and sent to a children's hospital, where Lakers players observed them metaphorically and literally hanging over their heads when they made subsequent charitable visits.

"It was a challenge to play against Russell and the Celtics," said Baylor. "It was fun. It was disappointing to lose. But it was the ultimate challenge. They were a proud team, and they had reason

"GREED...IS GOOD."

The look and wardrobe of Michael Douglas's Gordon Gekko character in *Wall Street* was based partly on Pat Riley. Riley also studied military history, using Sun Tzu's *The Art of War* to glean lessons just as Gekko and his protégé, Bud Fox (Charlie Sheen) did.

to be. Some people thought they were proud and arrogant. But I enjoyed playing against them. They were the best."

A FITTING MATCH

Sometimes just the right combination of people comes along to form something perfect. Can anybody imagine *The Godfather* starring anyone but Al Pacino and Marlon Brando? Would *Butch Cassidy and the Sundance Kid* have been the same hit without Robert Redford and Paul Newman?

The Los Angeles Lakers of the 1980s had just such a fitting match of talents and personalities. The anchor was Kareem Abdul-Jabbar, who had arrived in 1975 but performed in splendid agony for several seasons—MVPs, scoring titles, no championships.

Magic Johnson complemented Kareem just right, his enthusiasm overcoming any jealousy the Big Guy might have felt about somebody stealing his thunder. At the same time it allowed him to mellow and "outlive my critics," as he put it.

Then there was the coach. Jack McKinney may have been a good one, but we will never know. He was injured riding his bicycle and that was that. Paul Westhead was a good coach. He took Los Angeles to one NBA championship and later engineered little Loyola Marymount to great heights. But Westhead and Magic did not get along. Magic was copacetic with almost everybody, so that says something about Westhead. On that team at that time, you *had* to get along with Magic.

A great coach is not always just the guy who takes a struggling, undermanned team and leads it well beyond its normal abilities. Great coaches come in all shapes and sizes, possessing many strengths and specialties. At the college level, a coach might be great mainly as a recruiter. Some are organizers, motivators, defensive specialists, passing gurus. Some play "little ball," others wait for the "three-run homer." Some yell and throw things. Others are quiet, bookish, or reserved.

Do they win? That is the key. John Wooden and Bobby Knight were as different as night and day, but their teams won in similar manner: good defense, fundamentals, high graduation rates.

The simple fact is that when presented with a roster of great talent at the professional level in any sport, *most coaches* manage to screw it up. History is filled with teams of great expectations who failed. Tony LaRussa managed some of the most talented baseball teams in recent memory but won only one of three World Series with the 1988–90 Oakland A's. Throughout his career he fell short despite more great teams in St. Louis, but in 2006 the least of any of his clubs found the right chemistry and won it all.

Therefore, it is instructive to understand that just as impressive as Jim Leyland was leading Detroit out of nowhere in 2006 or Jim Valvano finding the upset formula at North Carolina State in 1983, the guy who takes superstars and gets them to win as superstars is perhaps doing an even better job of coaching.

Case in point: the Los Angeles Lakers. In the 1960s Fred Schaus, Bill van Breda Kolff, and Joe Mullaney had teams with the best talent in the NBA. Van Breda Kolff's 1968–69 West-Baylor-Chamberlain triumvirate was unheard of. They failed. Van Breda Kolff faded into the memory banks of basketball history.

Then Bill Sharman came along, the "man with the plan" in 1971–72. Greatness followed. So it was with Pat Riley, the handsome genius with the Armani suits and the slicked-back hair who represented L.A. style in the stylish '80s. Surrounded by talent, ego, money, sex, celebrity, and every conceivable distraction, he kept a team of young, testosterone-injected superstars—guys with all the money, women, and fame in the world—and got them to display the discipline of a Buckingham Palace guard.

He won in 1982, and that could well have been it. The competition was fierce. Boston was just as good: Larry Bird, Kevin McHale. Philadelphia might have been better: Julius Erving, Moses Malone. Either of those teams, Boston in particular, could have made a dynasty in the 1980s. Detroit could have started their run a year or two earlier. Instead of being a one-shot wonder in a town that breeds them, he got the Lakers to do what they needed to win year after year until it was *their* decade.

Riley starred at Linton High School in upstate New York. The highlight of his career was a holiday tournament victory over Power Memorial Academy of Manhattan. Riley outscored Power

Memorial's freshman center, Lew Alcindor, 19–8 (a fact he reminded Kareem Abdul-Jabbar of about once a week for a decade).

From there, Riley starred at Kentucky, where he was a member of the 1966 all-white Wildcats team that lost to Texas Western in the NCAA championship game. Texas Western was the first team to start five black players in the Final Four. That and the 1970 USC-Alabama football game, when the integrated Trojans beat the segregated Crimson Tide at Legion Field, are credited with opening the South to African Americans.

Riley played for the Lakers and other teams—a role player his whole career—then settled into broadcasting. His ascension to the job of Lakers coach, a job he did not pursue and probably was not qualified for, was one of great irony. It first involved coach Jack McKinney's head injury and then Paul Westhead's meltdown

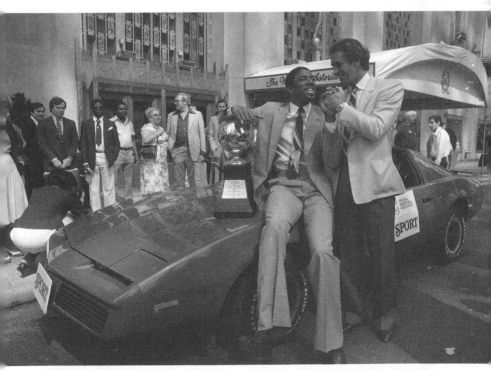

When the inwardly old-school but outwardly stylish Pat Riley arrived in the early 1980s to coach Magic Johnson and his talented teammates, it was a match made in Tinseltown that led to four Lakers titles.

leading to the fatal argument with Magic that cost him his job (and probably some major regrets). But Riley was in.

"I didn't know how to lead people," he said of that 1981–82 season. "So I read and I talked to people in leadership positions. I had to work."

The story could have ended in predictable fashion. First, injuries and disappointment in 1983, a year in which nobody was going to beat Philadelphia. Then 1984, when "we had the best team and flat-out choked when we lost to Boston."

Memory plays tricks, kindling the notion that in the 1980s Riley's teams won consistently and his players performed brilliantly. Magic, in fact, was accused of choking in 1984. Kareem was thought to be selfish. After the 1985 "Boston Massacre," a 148–114 Game 1 Celtics win, the Lakers' backs were to the wall. Then they won Game 2.

"That was the most significant game this team ever played," he said. "If we had lost, I'm sure I'd have been fired and people traded...it was the ultimate backs against the wall...and it brought out the best."

Riley's comments are significant. The team won, and therefore the Lakers stayed together: coach, superstars, role players. It was the chemistry experiment that allowed the whole team to gel perfectly.

In 1987 he guaranteed a repeat. When the Lakers became the first team since the 1968–69 Celtics to accomplish the feat, his role in history was secure. Riley coached other teams, but his reputation for motivating and leading was forged in L.A.

Had he done what he did—four titles in seven years—anyplace else, it would have been remarkable, but outside of maybe New York, doing it in the showtime atmosphere of Los Angeles was a truly remarkable feat. Just getting those Lakers to keep their minds on basketball instead of women was a major challenge. The players of that era were making huge money. The motivation of old no longer applied.

Riley was a contradiction, too. Despite his L.A. style, he was an old-school guy, grounded in winning ways.

THINGS TO SAVOR

SUPERSTAR

"He's either got three hands or two basketballs. It's like guarding a flood."

That was the assessment of former New York Knickerbocker Richie Guerin of Los Angeles Lakers superstar Elgin Baylor. Elgin was the first pick of the 1958 NBA draft. Before he came along, Boston's Bob Cousy demonstrated fancy ball-handling skills, but it is Baylor who is considered the forerunner of true *style* in pro basketball.

Baylor begat the likes of Rick Barry, Pete Maravich, Julius Erving, and Michael Jordan. He epitomized the new, modern game—the game that became so popular, a TV game, a glamour game.

For many years, Baylor's name was included on any "all-time NBA all-star team," and to this day purists do not like to leave his name off it. He was also a major player in the area of advancement for African American athletes in America. Basketball and football opened up after baseball had broken the color barrier with Jackie Robinson's entrance into the big leagues with Brooklyn in 1947. Many young black players, however, are not familiar with the path forged for them by the likes of Baylor, Bill Russell, and K.C. Jones.

"I tell black players today, there was a guy named Elgin Baylor," said Art Spander, who came out of UCLA, covered sports for the old *Santa Monica Evening Outlook*, and later became a columnist for the *San Francisco Examiner* and *Oakland Tribune*. "I still see Baylor and tell him, 'You don't know how good you were.'"

Baylor was born in 1934. His father took out his Elgin watch to note the time, and at the spur of the moment decided to name his son Elgin. Baylor grew up in Washington, D.C., and starred at Spingarn High School, where he was named to the All-Metropolitan team.

"He never shot much unless we needed points," said his coach, Dave Brown. "And even back then he was never excitable. In one big game, they got four quick fouls on him. I moved him outside and he made 44 points."

After high school Baylor played at the College of Idaho, where he averaged 31 points per game in 1954–55. When Idaho's basketball coach took the job at Seattle University after Baylor's freshman year, Baylor transferred in order to play for the Chieftains.

Baylor led the nation in rebounding with more than 20 boards per game, while averaging almost 30 points. In 1957–58 Baylor finished second behind Oscar Robertson in the NCAA with a 32.5 scoring average and was third with 19.3 rebounds, earning All-American honors while leading the 18th-ranked Chieftains to the NCAA title game before losing to Adolph Rupp's Kentucky Wildcats, 84–72. Baylor earned tournament outstanding player honors.

The Lakers, a troubled franchise that was on the verge of moving from Minneapolis to Los Angeles, chose Baylor with the first pick in 1958. Owner Bob Short signed Baylor to a $20,000-per-year deal. It was the signing of Baylor that encouraged him to hold on to the franchise instead of accepting an offer to sell the team. Potential buyers, however, fell below Short's $250,000 asking price. Seven years later, Jack Kent Cooke paid Short $5 million for the Lakers in Los Angeles.

"If he had turned me down then," recalled Short, "I'd have been out of business. The club would have been bankrupt."

But Baylor brought excitement and fan interest.

Elgin Baylor would go around, and through, defenses to get to the hole as he does here against the Knicks in 1970.

"When I went to training camp and saw all these big guys, I wondered if I really could make it," he recalled. "But right after the first practice, I could sense that I was as good as they were."

Baylor brought a new dimension to the NBA and was a sensation in his very first year. Prior to his emergence, the game was divided among players who performed fairly well-defined roles.

Big men roamed the post, blocking shots, making close-in baskets, and grabbing rebounds. Guards brought the ball up court and shot from the outside. The role of the forward, particularly the power forward, had not yet permeated the game's lexicon. Basketball, of course, is called a "noncontact sport," but this is a well-known misnomer. It was Baylor, however, who first defined the rugged physicality of his position.

Of course Elgin could shoot from the outside, but he loved to drive the lanes, using his size and quickness to his advantage. This not only made him a "scorer" in the nontraditional sense of the term, but it also helped him to draw fouls. This created a new dynamic, leading to opponents falling into foul trouble. It also gave his team an added offensive weapon in the closing minutes of contests, when they did not have to merely rely on outside shots to capture a game in the last moments but could draw fouls and therefore three-point plays.

Later players like Adrian Dantley took to the Baylor style. John Havlicek of the Celtics became his team's version of Baylor, preferring to drive to the hoop instead of taking the outside shot every time. Eventually, weight lifting came into popularity in basketball, with players using their strength to muscle in for shots and pound the boards.

Baylor had size, strength, and grace. He did not simply drive through defenses but demonstrated deft moves: head fakes, natural feints, misdirected foes. Before "Air Jordan," Baylor was a man who defied gravity.

Baylor won the Rookie of the Year award and earned All-Star Game MVP honors with Bob Pettit of the Hawks. Baylor was a proud man who earned his teammates' respect. He turned the

SOLDIER BOY

In 1961–62, Elgin Baylor missed many games because he was a member of an Army Reserve unit at Fort Lewis, Washington.

Lakers around, and in November he set a league record with 64 points in a game.

When the club moved to Los Angeles and Jerry West joined them, it was a major event. The urban African American Baylor and the rural Southerner West meshed perfectly, complementing each other on offense and defense. They were great players, and their teamwork on and off the court was a self-evident truth that improved race relations through sports. Los Angeles, the city of the future in the 1960s, was the perfect place for these two. Old stereotypes did not hold true with the West-Baylor partnership.

West was as physically gifted as Baylor. Baylor worked as hard as West. They were both team leaders in their own way, neither stepping on the other's toes. Baylor was vocal and dynamic, West more reserved. It was Wilt Chamberlain's presence eight years after West's arrival that caused problems, at least if the media were to be believed.

In Jerry's first year, Baylor scored 35 points per game. He broke his own record, garnering an incredible 71 points on November 15, 1960, against New York.

"It was just a typical Baylor performance," recalled the Knicks' Johnny Green.

Baylor was a master at getting the second shot, rebounding his own misses, and getting the extra opportunity—a talent many players, who prefer to watch their shot sail through the air spectator style, do not possess or care to do the hard work to achieve.

Baylor was not spectacular in the way that Rick Barry and Pete Maravich were. He just worked hard and never let up. When the game was over, a look at the stat sheet revealed another big game. West, the ace from outside, often garnered more attention. As great as Jerry was, neither West nor his teammates or coaches would say that West was more valuable.

In the early 1960s Baylor was drafted by the army but was made available to play on a part-time basis. He scored 61 points against Boston in 1962, a playoff record that broke Wilt Chamberlain's mark of 56 and held up until Michael Jordan's 63 in 1986. In the seventh game of that memorable series, Frank

Selvy's game-winning try missed and the Celtics captured the title in overtime.

In three of the following seasons, Los Angeles lost to Boston in the Finals. Baylor completed his military service and averaged 34 points in 1962–63. He and Oscar Robertson were the most complete players in the game. Chamberlain scored more. West was a better shooter. But Baylor scored, rebounded, dished off assists, and played strong defense.

In the 1965 playoffs against Baltimore, Baylor suffered the first of the debilitating injuries that eventually cut his effectiveness, and his career, short. It was his knee, and eventually he "just accepted the fact that [he] would never play again."

He did return, but according to announcer Chick Hearn, "It was like watching Citation [a Triple Crown horse-racing champion] run on spavined legs." Dr. Robert Kerlan was able to repair Baylor's knee enough to get him back sooner than previously expected. While he was never quite the phenom of his earliest years, he did regain much of his greatness. It was Dr. Kerlan's efforts with Baylor that vaulted the orthopedic surgeon to prominence and changed the nature of sports medicine. Baylor's knee was repaired enough to allow him to score 41 points in a playoff game with Boston.

"It was an amazing recovery, certainly," said Dr. Kerlan. "But only if you consider it simply overcoming an injury. The man is often the most important thing, and in view of the sort of man Elgin is, then maybe we should have expected it."

Over the next four seasons, Baylor averaged 25 points per game. West, who maintained good health throughout most of his career, became the dominant scorer on the team. When Chamberlain joined the team in 1968, the media immediately fixated on the relationship between he and Baylor. The "problem," which was that Wilt blocked the left lane where Baylor liked to drive, seemed to be more between Butch van Breda Kolff and Wilt than Baylor and Wilt. Baylor, the team guy, just wanted to win. However, Chamberlain's dominating personality did have an effect on Baylor. Elgin became less verbal, less the team leader. But when Wilt was injured throughout much of the 1969–70 season, Baylor picked up the slack on and off the court.

Baylor never found the need to make recriminations over the 1969 and 1970 playoff losses to Boston and New York, even though a great deal of blame was laid on Chamberlain. They were devastating defeats, but the three superstars—Baylor, West, and Chamberlain—were all still in or close to their prime when Baylor tore his Achilles tendon the next year.

The team floundered and was destroyed by Lew Alcindor and Oscar Robertson in the playoffs. That had to be extra salt in the wound for Chamberlain and West, natural rivals of Alcindor and Robertson. Baylor's injury seemed to confirm the notion that they were "cursed," or at the very least, star-crossed.

In 1971 Baylor tried to come back for one last try. Bill Sharman had taken over. He ran a style of offense tailor-made for a young Baylor. But the injury was this time impossible to overcome.

"I don't want to prolong my career to the time when I can't maintain [high standards]," Baylor told the media in announcing his retirement.

What happened next was bittersweet. Without him, the Lakers of West, Chamberlain, Gail Goodrich, Happy Hairston, and Jim McMillian rolled to the best season in pro basketball history up to that time. Their first NBA championship was won without Baylor, although technically he was a member of the team, having played the first nine games of the regular season before calling it quits.

The team tried to include him in their celebration, but Baylor knew that it was not real. The team shed its "can't win the big one" image, a sports moniker that at that time and in the preceding years had hung around the necks of the Oakland Raiders, Dallas Cowboys, and Los Angeles Rams. Baylor's injury put him in the same category as Oakland's Jim Otto and George Blanda, star players of Raiders lore who were forced to retire by physical limitations, only to see their team finally win the Super Bowl in their absence.

Ironically, the day Baylor retired Los Angeles defeated Baltimore 110–106, starting the greatest winning streak in pro sports history, 33 games. At the time of his retirement, Baylor was the third-highest scorer in NBA history. Only Chamberlain and

Michael Jordan topped his career scoring average of 27.4, although West's average dropped below that only because he played into the waning years of his great career.

Baylor averaged over 30 points in three seasons and made All-NBA 10 of 11 seasons. After retirement he got into coaching and was elected to the Hall of Fame. He was named to the NBA 50th Anniversary All-NBA Team. *Sports Illustrated* claimed that teammate Tommy Hawkins invented the term "superstar" in describing Baylor. He eventually became the executive vice president of the Los Angeles Clippers. Ironically Baylor, who had a taciturn way about him when dealing with the media, was criticized for his association with the poor Clippers teams, but as a Lakers player he was truly a superstar.

THE DEFINING MOMENT

They called it "Showtime," which coach Pat Riley said was basketball's "defining moment." That moment lasted a decade.

It all started not in Los Angeles but in Salt Lake City, Utah, on March 26, 1979. Sophomore Earvin "Magic" Johnson led Michigan State to the national championship over senior Larry Bird and Indiana State. Exactly why this matchup received so much attention, why it created the biggest television audience ever to tune into a college game (Michigan State versus Indiana State?) is somewhat mysterious. Obviously, Johnson and Bird had demonstrated extraordinary skills. People sensed that here were two new giants of the hardwood—one an urban black kid, the other a "hick from French Lick"—both possessing not just court skills but a kind of charisma that, at least back then, could not really be defined.

"To me, what that game means," Magic told Fox Sports' Chris Myers in a 2006 retrospective, "is that I got one up on Larry. He's one of the greatest players who ever lived, but I got one up on him. He'll tell you it hurts him to this day, because we're both winners and hate losing, so I got this one on him."

"That game still hurts," Bird agreed. "It isn't the losing, it's that so many people in Indiana were behind us and it didn't happen."

INJURY FRONT

Elgin Baylor's Achilles injury in 1971 forced his retirement, allowing Bill Sharman to install the fast-break offense he preferred. The Lakers immediately won 33 straight games on the way to their first NBA title in Los Angeles.

Johnson's persona was easier to identify with. He was good-looking with an infectious smile and sunny personality. Bird was different. He mumbled and was nobody's idea of a matinee idol. Admit it or not, though, he was the "great white hope" in a game that had been dominated by black players and an unfortunate criminal/drug element in the previous decade.

Johnson and Michigan State beat Bird and Indiana State that night, but like the 2006 Rose Bowl football game featuring Texas's Vince Young versus USC's Matt Leinart, Reggie Bush, and LenDale White, there were no real losers. Noble defeat only foreshadowed future duels, which promised to be a battle of giants for years to come.

It saved the National Basketball Association. Johnson was drafted number one by the Lakers and awarded $600,000. His enthusiasm spread from the beginning and probably revived Kareem Abdul-Jabbar's career.

The *Showtime* moniker came from Buss. Los Angeles is a traditional city, although this might surprise some. But its roots are somewhat Confederate and Midwestern. Southerners looking for opportunity in California chose it over San Francisco, the preferred destination of Abe Lincoln's railroad and all those "damn Yankees" from Boston. The Rose Bowl drew so many people from the heartland that *Los Angeles Times* sports columnist Jim Murray called Long Beach "Iowa by the Sea."

That was the way of the Forum, too. The Hollywood crowd of course flocked there, as they did to Chavez Ravine, but it was staid and organ-music slow. But Jerry Buss was a modern guy—a ladies' man who liked the clubs, the party scene, and hip music. In the

With Magic and coach Pat Riley at the peak of their careers in the 1980s, Showtime became one of the must-see events in jaded Los Angeles.

1960s he hung out at a nightclub on Wilshire Boulevard in Santa Monica called The Horn.

The club featured an opening act in which the lights would dim, the spotlights would come up, and then a singer would emerge from one of the tables announcing, "It's *showtime!*" Then two rows stood and created harmony. When Buss bought the Lakers, he already knew that he wanted this same kind of buildup to replace the organ grinder at the Forum.

In 1979–80, after coach Jack McKinney suffered a head injury that required assistant Paul Westhead to replace him, the team jelled perfectly. They won 60 games behind the Most Valuable Player efforts of Kareem Abdul-Jabbar.

In the East, Bird led Boston to 61 wins, earning Rookie of the Year honors over Magic. Fans and media were still adjusting to Johnson's playing style. With Bird it was all there: tenacious defense, dead-eye shooting, 21 points per game. Johnson took some getting used to. At 6'9" nobody had ever seen a guard that tall (although early on he was at forward), but he handled the ball like a six-footer. His height gave him the advantage when it came to finding the open man, his specialty. He did not score like Bird, so to the naked eye he did not at first look as spectacular. He could score, as opposed to being a pure shooter, but he gained assists by the bushel and pulled down rebounds. He was a floor general like none before, and this included the likes of Bob Cousy. Magic would stand almost sideways, his back to the defense, hiding the dribbled basketball. Then he would use his height to fire a bullet pass over the heads of opponents to a streaking man near the basket.

Magic and Kareem negotiated Los Angeles into the NBA Finals against Dr. J and Philadelphia, who had knocked off Boston. For several years, television viewership was so bad that the Finals, including this one, were tape-delayed. However, this series was a ratings hit, and the tape delay would be dropped after one more season.

Kareem dominated the post. Norm Nixon and Jamaal Wilkes were spectacular, and Magic was the spark plug igniting the whole engine. Sixth man Michael Cooper occasionally ran the backcourt so Magic could move to power forward when Westhead saw that the Sixers were literally in over their heads under the basket. The teams split the first two games. Kareem's 33 points gave them a Game 3 victory.

Philadelphia played tough, tying it 2–2 at home. In a memorable Game 5 at the Forum, Kareem was dominating when he twisted his ankle. In a desperate move Magic took over at center, of all positions, holding his own until Abdul-Jabbar could return. L.A. held on for a key 108–103 victory.

Game 6 at the Philadelphia Spectrum was played without Kareem, whose injury worsened in the aftermath of the game. Magic was again asked to play center, a position he had played in high school.

"Paul's fear was that we couldn't match up with Darryl Dawkins and Caldwell Jones," Johnson recalled. "I told him I could play Caldwell Jones, and he looked at me like, 'Jesus, he's seven feet tall!' He couldn't believe that I could match up. I told him, 'Coach, on the other end, what are they gonna do with us? Who's gonna guard the guys we have?'"

Abdul-Jabbar rested for the presumed Game 7 in L.A. He did not even make the trip to Philadelphia. Magic put himself in Kareem's shoes, so to speak. He sat in Kareem's seat on the plane, stretched through Kareem's normal routine, then pulled a blanket over his head as Abdul-Jabbar liked to do.

His legend would be made that night.

Up until game time the 76ers still thought Abdul-Jabbar's absence was a ruse. There were "Kareem sightings" reported in the Philadelphia media. Coach Billy Cunningham was thinking he would come through the tunnel even after the game began. Memories of Willis Reed's unexpected appearance at Madison Square Garden 10 years earlier were rekindled.

In the years since, many of the Lakers admitted they did not think they had a chance without their center and captain. When L.A. raced to 7–0 and 11–4 leads, all bets were off, though. Then the Sixers forged ahead, 52–44, in the second quarter. Los Angeles tied it at 60 by halftime and then scored the first 14 points of the third quarter. Wilkes poured in 16.

Magic refused to let the team wilt. After withstanding a late 76er run, he scored nine points down the stretch to secure an improbable 123–107 win and the club's second NBA title. He scored 42, including 14-of-14 from the free throw line, pulled down 15 rebounds playing center against men four inches taller than he was, and had a block, three steals, and seven assists. All in all, it goes down in history as one of the finest performances ever.

"It was amazing, just amazing," said Dr. J.

"Magic was outstanding. Unreal," said Philadelphia guard Doug Collins. "I knew he was good, but I never realized he was this great."

Johnson won the series MVP award and addressed Kareem through the TV camera, telling him he expected him to be "dancing" with the rest of them when they got back home.

"We'll be partyin' in L.A.," Magic said with a twinkle in his eye. Fans just fantasized what *that* would be like. His reputation as a fun-loving guy who had a way with beautiful women was already well-known. As for Kareem, he handled it his way: poorly. He was bitter that he had not won the MVP and that so much credit went to Magic.

"My game was the foundation which enabled James and Earvin and Byron and Norman and all these guys to do their thing on the perimeter while I created what I created inside," he said in Roland Lazenby's *The Lakers: A Basketball Journey.*

This was, of course, all true. Without him the Lakers of that era may not have won any titles, and certainly not five, but Abdul-Jabbar had been a Laker for four years prior to Magic's arrival without a title, or even a Finals appearance. Prior to that he had been a Buck for four years without a championship. Overall, Kareem had been in the NBA a decade with one championship to his credit. That had occurred after Oscar Robertson joined forces with him.

His assessment of the media, the fans, and the credit he got for his team's success is misguided. He was unpopular because he was unfriendly, but anybody who knew anything always recognized his greatness on the court. Magic was popular because he was an engaging figure. While his team's success undoubtedly came about in large measure because of Kareem and other excellent players, it would be wrong to assess Magic as anything less than a truly great player, above all but the most elite of basketball legends. Many find it sacrilegious to state it, but the record indicates that Johnson was simply better even than Jerry West, and it does not get better than that.

Abdul-Jabbar's contention that he should have won the 1980 Finals MVP award is a selfish assessment. He claimed correctly that he got his team into position to beat Philadelphia. For the first four or five games he *was* the MVP. But he watched the sixth game on TV while Magic Johnson rose to the occasion in a manner comparable to Reggie Jackson in the 1977 World Series, or Johnny Unitas in the 1958 NFL championship game. The graceful thing he should have said, instead of spouting conspiracy theories about how the league wanted the award to go to Johnson on TV instead of to an absent Abdul-Jabbar, was "Congratulations...wow!"

Larry Bird and Boston claimed the 1981 NBA title. In 1981–82 Magic and Westhead argued, and the resulting furor led to Westhead's immediate firing. This must gnaw at Westhead to this day, when one considers what he helped start and could have been a part of had he been there throughout the decade. Of course, the whole scenario—Jerry Tarkanian's bizarre nonhiring, Jack McKinney's injury, Westhead's firing, and Pat Riley's subsequent deification—brings into question the fickle hand of fate.

Johnson was a superstar and the future. He had to be kept happy. He proved himself to be a leader, a great teammate, a player who was admired and loved. If he did not get along with Westhead, Westhead deserves some blame, although probably not all. But ultimately he was not going to win a power struggle with Magic Johnson.

With Riley taking over on November 19, 1981, L.A. won 17 of their next 20 games. Mitch Kupchak injured his leg and was replaced by Bob McAdoo. Los Angeles compiled a 57–25 mark for first place in the Pacific Division. As if to prove that 1980 was no fluke, Magic Johnson was again the MVP of the NBA Finals. Abdul-Jabbar was slowly ceding his status as the team's greatest superstar, but he still averaged 24 points a game to lead in scoring.

Wilkes hit for 21, Magic 19, Norm Nixon 18, and Michael Cooper 12 points a game.

They again vanquished Philadelphia in the Finals by four games to two. The 1980s may have been the greatest decade in NBA history. Aside from the Lakers-Celtics rivalry, the Lakers-Sixers rivalry was hot and heated. In 1983 Philadelphia, with Moses Malone, compiled one of the best years in Association annals, capturing the title.

By 1984, the two marquee superstars in the National Basketball Association were Magic Johnson and Larry Bird. Each had been in the league four full years, with Magic winning two NBA championships and Bird one.

Kareem Abdul-Jabbar was still a force, but age was catching up to him. It was Magic's team. In Philadelphia, the 1983 championship was a last hurrah of sorts for Dr. J and Malone. The stage was set for the next great battle of titans in professional sports.

Bird and Johnson followed each other closely. Their 1979 college bout had tied them together. They were both fans of the game who read the papers, checked the stats, and enjoyed the exploits of the other. They were rivals but seemed disposed to friendship, both of them pleasant and likable in their own way.

NUMBERS DON'T LIE (OR DO THEY?)

27.4—Elgin Baylor's career scoring average (1960–71).

Lakers' Retired Numbers
13—Wilt Chamberlain
22—Elgin Baylor
25—Gail Goodrich
32—Magic Johnson
33—Kareem Abdul-Jabbar
42—James Worthy
44—Jerry West

In 1984 the matchup everybody had been anticipating since 1979 came to fruition. As Scott Ostler and Steve Springer pointed out in *Winnin' Times* (named after Magic's favorite expression), the rivalry mirrored the USC–Notre Dame tradition with some professional dazzle thrown in. But the Lakers-Celtics rivalry took on a new dimension in the 1980s. Black stars dominated the Celtics of the 1950s and '60s. Two white players, Bird and Kevin McHale, dominated the 1980s Celtics.

The Lakers were a team of African American superstars. White fans identified with Boston, black fans with Los Angeles, but this dynamic never took on ugly overtones. Magic and Bird were so classy, such noble competitors, that the kind of societal dynamics that might have marred the proceedings never happened.

"The number one thing is desire," Bird said. "The ability to do the things you have to do to become a basketball player. I don't think you can teach anyone desire. I think it's a gift. I don't know why I have it, but I do."

James Worthy had joined the Lakers out of North Carolina. He got into verbal battles with Bird on the floor.

"You can't guard me," Bird would taunt him. At first it threw Worthy, but he came to realize it was just gamesmanship.

"He could tell if your confidence wasn't right," Worthy said. "He could sense the vibe," and if he was not met with aggressiveness, "he had you."

In the years preceding the 1984 Finals, the league's TV rights money had grown from the tape delays of the 1970s, eventually going from $14 million to $100 million. Bird was embarking on his greatest years: three straight MVP awards from 1984 to 1986. Perhaps even more impressive was the incredible—albeit biased— declaration from Red Auerbach that he had replaced Bill Russell as the greatest player of all time. Wilt Chamberlain countered that Magic was the best. Bird on Magic? "He's the perfect player." It was a statement Russell never would have made of Wilt, or vice versa, at least not in their playing days. Off the court, there was mutual respect between Bird and Magic, but on the court, competition could lead to heated confrontation.

Los Angeles overcame injuries and question marks, and they finished in dominant fashion, winning 41 of their last 56 games. This included rolling through Kansas City, Dallas, and Phoenix to get to the Finals. On to Boston and "weirdness," according to Worthy, who described reminders of the "jinx": fire alarms in the hotel, humidity in Boston Garden, and "external things." Auerbach was accused of sending warm air into the Lakers dressing room to increase the humidity.

He did "dastardly things" and was "classless," said Magic's agent, Lon Rosen.

Los Angeles was so talented, so loaded, it seemed nothing could stop them, not even one of Kareem's migraines, which bothered him throughout the years. The 37-year-old Abdul-Jabbar still scored 32 points with two blocks, leading L.A. to a 115–109 win at the Garden. The jinx looked dead.

But that notion was revived in a big way in Game 2 when James Worthy's 29 points were overshadowed by the fact that his team, which was firmly in control throughout, suddenly blew the lead late in the game. Inexplicably, the Lakers stood around on offense, as if they were waiting for somebody—Magic, Kareem, Worthy?—to take charge. No one did. It was one of the worst games in Lakers history. Worthy, after performing heroically all day, telegraphed a pass into the hands of Boston's Gerald Henderson. Instead of Los Angeles sweeping to a 2–0 lead, Boston had life and a tie after their 124–121 win.

At the Forum, Johnson had one of his greatest games, getting an unreal 21 assists in a 137–104 blowout. In Game 4, L.A. threatened to run away with it, but Boston coach K.C. Jones instructed his team to get more physical. Boston became "a bunch of thugs," said Riley. Kevin McHale clotheslined Kurt Rambis, but the Lakers still led by five with three minutes to play in front of the home fans. Then Robert Parish stole a Johnson pass and Magic missed two key free throws, forcing overtime. Boston won 129–125. If Game 2 was the worst in Lakers history, Game 4 replaced it. Instead of a 3–1 series lead, it was 2–2 with a trip to Boston and more "external distractions" ahead of them. It was similar in nature to the 1960 World Series, in which the Yankees won three games by blowouts but lost four close calls to Pittsburgh, the world champions.

Game 5 at the Garden was the so-called heat game, with the Lakers sucking out of an oxygen tank on the bench in 97-degree indoor temperatures. The psychology was overwhelming, as were Bird—15 of 20, 34 points—and the Celtics, who won by 121–103. Kareem seemed old, completely unable to deal with the conditions. Bird just smiled and said it was like playing on asphalt courts in the summer.

But Kareem scored 30 in L.A. to tie it up. Boston had the seventh game at home and led by 14 until a late L.A. surge closed it to three with a minute to go. The ball was in Magic Johnson's hands. Dennis Johnson knocked it loose. The Lakers recovered it. Cedric Maxwell knocked it out of Magic's hand *again*. In the end it was 111–102. In the professional battle between Bird and Magic it was round one to Larry, Boston's 15th NBA title, and eight-for-eight against the Lakers since 1962.

"Whatever happened to that Laker dynasty I've been hearing so much about?" Auerbach chortled in the winning Boston dressing room.

The Boston fans were classless and borderline violent outside the Garden. The Lakers exit was like something out of *Black Hawk Down*. It was so bad they could not get out of town, forced to hole up in the hotel as if they were fugitives. They had blown it. They were the better team, and they would learn the emotional lessons of this defeat.

The 1984–85 Lakers came out from the very first day of training camp in Palm Springs resolved to avenge the defeat. The Celtics and the Los Angeles papers hounded them unmercifully throughout the off-season, giving them more resolve, as if they needed it. The Lakers went 62–20. Mitch Kupchak and Jamaal Wilkes bolstered Kareem, Worthy, Rambis, Bob McAdoo, and Larry Spriggs down low, with Magic, Byron Scott, Michael Cooper, and Mike McGee in the backcourt.

"Those wounds from last June stayed all summer," Riley explained. The coach thought the 25-year-old Magic had matured,

JOURNEYMAN

Kurt Rambis was a 6'8" power forward from the University of Santa Clara who was an integral member of the Showtime Lakers from 1981 to 1988. He later played for Los Angeles from 1993 to 1995 and was even their coach at the end of the 1998–99 season.

realizing the onus was on him. He was sensitive to the criticism and hoped to atone for it.

But Boston had a better record by a game and earned the Garden advantage. They took care of Cleveland, Detroit, and Philadelphia. L.A. dispatched Phoenix, Portland, and Denver. It was the sports version of England versus Germany in 1940, a rematch of World War II proportions. Call it the "Battle of Boston." After the Celtics' 148–114 blowout in Game 1, it started to look like the blitzkrieg. The Lakers, like England, would have to respond with their version of El Alamein when the war shifted to the desert, which is essentially what the L.A. Basin is.

The format was now like baseball: two games in Boston, three in L.A., two in Boston, if it went all the way. After the embarrassment of Game 1, Kareem decided to take charge. He asserted himself as the team leader and asked Riley if his father could ride on the team bus from the hotel. Normally Riley would have had none of it, but he used the opportunity to invite Mr. Alcindor into the team's inner circle. Riley made a speech about his own father, who, when Pat was getting beat up as a kid, had urged him to keep fighting because, "You have to make a stand." That was the theme of Riley's motivational talk. It worked for a seven-point win that reversed Boston momentum in front of the home fans, who had come out for blood.

In Los Angeles the Lakers smacked Boston 136–111 behind Worthy's 29 points and Kareem's 14 rebounds. Bird was defended well. In Game 4, the NBA had to warn the teams that their physical play was getting out of hand. In that atmosphere the proud Celtics tied the series with a 107–105 win, ensuring a trip back

East and home-court advantage. It was Magic who took control at the end of Game 5, a 120–111 Forum win that sent the teams to Beantown with Los Angeles holding a 3–2 edge. However, to blow that lead and lose at the Garden was a distinct possibility. It would fall in line with the history of the rivalry, which, at least up until 1985, was beginning to look less like a rivalry and more like domination.

The score was tied, 55–55 at the half. Again Magic handled the second half on both ends of the floor to spur his team to a 111–100 win. For the first time, Boston fans had to sit in silence listening to the squeak of sneakers and the shouts of their victorious opponents, the 1985 world champion Lakers.

This time it was Kareem, not Magic, who took home the MVP award. Unlike Kareem, Magic was more than happy to share the glory. They visited President Ronald Reagan at the White House and then flew home. It was sweet redemption.

In 1986 the team could have used one of the slaves the Roman emperor Caesar had employed to constantly whisper in his ear, "All glory is fleeting." They lacked chemistry and fell in the first round to Houston. Boston in turn defeated the Rockets and won the championship. However, 1986 had the same effect as the 1984 loss at Boston. It refocused them on getting back to the Promised Land.

The '86 loss to Houston also redirected the team toward Magic. Abdul-Jabbar actually took the blame for the loss to Ralph Sampson, which was an act of maturity as well as acknowledgment that at 40 years old in 1986–87, the team needed to prepare for his inevitable retirement. While Magic was arguably the team leader before the season, he was undoubtedly "the Man" beginning that year.

Johnson had a fabulous season, earning league MVP, averaging 24 points and 12 assists per game. Young A.C. Green, a second-year player, was a shot in the arm, both on and off the court. The Lakers of that era lived up to their Showtime image. They were socializers who enjoyed the party scene. Green, a devout Christian who made his vow of abstinence a very public thing, did not prevent Magic and his cohorts from enjoying themselves, but he did add an aura of personal discipline to the proceedings that certainly did not hurt. The fact that he was a top-flight player was of great value, too.

At midseason the Lakers aquired 6'10" Mychal Thompson from San Antonio. Privately, Larry Bird acknowledged that his team could not overcome that. A teammate of McHale's at the University of Minnesota, Thompson knew how to stop the Celtics' power forward in the playoffs. At 65–17, the Lakers entered the postseason bidding to become one of the greatest teams ever—better than the '85 world champions.

In 1987 it was Michael Cooper's superior defensive skills that were spotlighted, and defense wins championships. He was a hard worker who spent hours studying Larry Bird on videotape. When the game started, Bird did not give the same kind of verbal taunts to Cooper. He knew he did not have the best of him. Cooper simply said, "Nothing tonight, Larry."

In 1987 Los Angeles cruised through the Western playoff rounds while Boston had to fight past the up-and-coming Detroit Pistons. Boston arrived at the Forum, where L.A. had the home-court advantage throughout the series, bruised but relatively confident. The comparison of the two teams reached its height at this time: the image of Bird and McHale as blue-collar players and the portrayal of the Lakers as naturally "better athletes."

Pat Riley would have none of it. He put his team through the paces with too much effort and preparation to accept that they just glided to victory. He also knew that in the playoffs, the hardest-working team would beat the more athletic one. He was bound and determined that his team would not be outworked.

An obstacle to Riley's focused approach was all the celebrity glitz at the Forum, where a galaxy of stars like never before made their way to courtside. Riley was worried that their appearance would have the effect of softening the Lakers. He made a point of calling them a "bunch of glitter-group, superficial laidbacks" and "empty people," contrasting them with a Lakers team that he declared was "the hardest-working team I've ever had."

But Boston came in dog-tired from fending off Dennis Rodman, Isiah Thomas, and the young Detroit "Bad Boys." The

---

QUOTE

"The way I look at my role as a floor leader is to remember that it's some-times more important how you say things on the court than what you actually say.... Tensions can get pretty high on a basketball court..."
—Magic Johnson, 1989

---

rested Johnson had 29 points and 13 assists, mostly to Worthy (33 points), while pulling down eight rebounds in a 126–113 L.A. rout.

In Game 2, Boston held Magic in check, but Kareem hit for 23 and Cooper took over to spur a 141–122 win that hinted at a sweep. Boston held on to avoid that, 109–103. In Game 4, Bird hit a three-pointer with 12 seconds left to give Boston a 106–104 lead, to the delight of the home crowd. Kareem was then fouled, making the first shot but missing the second. McHale grabbed the rebound, but Thompson knocked it out of bounds. The referee signaled that it had been touched by McHale last. L.A. ball. Loud booing.

Magic took the in-bounds pass, thought about a shot, and then moved around McHale into the key where Bird and Parish met him. Magic threw up a perfect hook shot, *swish*, and after Bird missed Boston's last chance, it was over, 107–106 Lakers.

"That's the year Pat said, 'Okay, Earvin, I want you to take over,'" recalled Johnson. "And that's what happened. After that, people said, 'It is Larry *and* Magic,' instead of, 'Larry can do this, and Magic can't do that.' You always had to fight that."

After the game, Auerbach again demonstrated classlessness by chasing referee Earl Strom into the dressing room like a recalci-trant child.

"You expect to lose on a skyhook," Bird told reporters. "You don't expect it to be Magic."

Bird and Boston were no match for Los Angeles, but they were a disciplined group of professionals. They staved off defeat with a 123–108 win. The Celtics even led Game 6 at the Forum by five points at the half, but Worthy and Kareem combined for 54 points, many coming on Magic's 19 assists. Los Angeles earned the NBA title and legitimate comparison with the greatest teams ever with a six-game series win, 106–93. Bird conceded that Magic was "the best I've ever seen."

Riley agreed. Johnson added that the '87 Lakers were the best team he had ever played for. Both admitted that the 1984 Lakers should have won that series and that the 1985 Lakers were a great team, but they felt the 1987 Lakers were deeper and better than any of the previous champions. No sooner did the Lakers capture the 1987 title than Pat Riley was asked about his team's chance at a repeat.

"I guarantee it," he announced.

It was the most brazen prediction since Joe Namath had done the same thing prior to beating the Baltimore Colts in the 1969 Super Bowl. But Riley's players thought he was crazy. In a game so filled with emotion, and when the road to a repeat might very well have to go back through Boston, they envisioned fighting Riley's words as much as opponents. The last repeat champions were the 1968–69 Celtics, but Riley, the master motivator, had a method to his madness. The Lakers of 1981, 1983, and 1986 had all failed to follow titles with intense repeat performances. He wanted to mix it up and give them something to fight for, even if he and his team would be under added pressure. Roland Lazenby in *The Lakers: A Basketball Journey*, described Riley as "a man obsessed. He was Captain Ahab..." in 1987–88. The result was victory again.

Just as Riley had assigned extra duties of responsibility to Magic, so too did he do the same with Worthy, an emerging superstar who was asked to pick up much of the pace that the 41-year-old Abdul-Jabbar would not be able to maintain. At 6'9" he was a power player but also fast enough to run the speed game.

Byron Scott scored almost 22 points a game. A.C. Green rebounded well and played great defense. Thompson replaced the tired Kareem at key times. The team started 8–0 and Showtime was in full swing. But there were injuries, and if they were to be stopped this would be the cause. But in the end Riley pushed them, and their depth was paramount in a sterling 62–20 record.

"Guaranteeing a championship was the best thing Pat ever did," Byron Scott said as the season wore to a close.

The playoffs were a challenge. After San Antonio fell three games to none, Los Angeles had to win three straight seven-game series on the way to the title. Karl Malone and Utah, Dallas, then Detroit's Bad Boys all played them to the seventh game before succumbing.

Isiah Thomas led Detroit past Boston and into the Finals. Adrian Dantley spurred the Pistons to a 105–93 win in front of a shocked Forum crowd, but as usual it was Johnson who righted the ship with 23 points to a key Game 2 victory, 108–96.

Forty thousand fans packed the Pontiac Silverdome, a football stadium, for Game 3. L.A. stifled Detroit in a 99–86 win to regain control. Dennis Rodman became extra physical in Game 4, and Detroit evened things at two. When this tactic continued in a 104–94 Game 5 Pistons win, L.A. was looking at elimination.

As Hal Holbrook said in that year's hit movie *Wall Street*, "When you're staring into the pit, you find your character. And that's what keeps you out of the pit." The Lakers found their character, but first Thomas put on one of the game's great displays in Los Angeles, pushing, cajoling, and willing his team to a three-point lead with just a minute left to play. The league trophy was wheeled into the Pistons dressing room. Iced champagne, too. CBS called Detroit owner Bill Davidson, telling him to be ready to accept the trophy.

But Byron Scott hit a 14-foot jumper to narrow it to one with 52 seconds to play. Thomas missed from outside against aggressive defense. Abdul-Jabbar got the ball and went for a skyhook, which was unstoppable. Bill Laimbeer had no choice but to foul him and hope he missed from the line. Kareem hit both, and it was 103–102, Los Angeles. A Detroit miss and Rodman's inability to grab the rebound ended things, and it was on to the seventh game.

Thomas, who had injured himself, was unable to compete effectively past the third quarter, when Los Angeles took a 90–75 lead. The crowd got into it, but the hubris left everybody off guard enough to let the Pistons back into the game. Magic managed to control things just enough at the end. The Lakers had their repeat, 108–105.

Worthy scored 36 and earned series MVP honors. Riley did not actually predict a "three-peat," but he did copyright the phrase. Because of this, 17 years later another Los Angeles sports team, the Southern California Trojans, were prevented from marketing variations of the theme "three-*Pete*" (a riff on coach Pete Carroll's name). The 2005 Trojans were marching toward what looked to be the first-ever third-straight AP national championship in college football until Texas beat them in the Rose Bowl.

These Lakers would not win another title, but Showtime was not officially over. In 1989 Kareem retired, and his tour of the league was a wonderful sendoff. Magic and Bird continued to be star players. But in 1989 the Bad Boys could not be stopped, blowing Los Angeles out in four straight.

The 1989–90 Lakers were a force to be reckoned with, winning 63 regular-season games before getting knocked out by Phoenix in the playoffs. Chuck Daly's Pistons captured a "repeat" of their own that season. In 1991 the overachieving Lakers made it to the Finals, but it was the beginning of Michael Jordan and the Bulls dynasty. Chicago won in five games.

It was the end of an era—an era of Showtime, the height of the Lakers-Celtics and Magic-Larry rivalry, and of consistently exciting NBA Finals. The league had managed to harness the excitement of Showtime by riding Johnson's popularity, but in

INJURY FRONT

One of the worst injuries the Lakers ever sustained occurred not to a player but to coach Jack McKinney. Hired after the Jerry Tarkanian fiasco, 13 games into the 1979–80 season McKinney had Magic Johnson's first team at 9–4. He was riding his bicycle to a tennis appointment in Westwood when he suffered an accident that caused a severe head injury. McKinney had to be replaced by assistant coach Paul Westhead. Ex-Laker Pat Riley, doing color commentary with Chick Hearn in the announcer's booth, was made an assistant coach.

November 1991 it all ended for the Lakers—symbolically and literally—when Magic announced he was HIV-positive.

In many ways 1988 was the last great year in Los Angeles until the 2000s. The Dodgers won the World Series in '88. Collegiately, USC and UCLA were unbeaten until mid-November with both teams vying for the national championship and the Heisman Trophy (Rodney Peete versus Troy Aikman). After this season, however, there would be a decline in the city on and off the fields of play.

In 1991 a video camera caught white L.A.P.D. officers beating a black motorist, Rodney King. Their subsequent not guilty verdicts from an all-white jury in the L.A. suburbs caused riots in 1992.

With the cold war won, the so-called Military Industrial Complex no longer was required to make bigger and better weapons to match the Soviet Union. The aerospace industry, probably the biggest slice of the Los Angeles workforce, had to lay off thousands of high-tech employees. The result was a major downturn in the California economy of the early 1990s.

Southern California had always dominated state politics, but in 1992 two Democrats from San Francisco, Barbara Boxer and Dianne Feinstein, were elected to the U.S. Senate in what came to be known as the "Year of the Woman."

In 1994 an earthquake rocked the Southland. That year, O.J. Simpson's wife and her friend Ron Goldman were murdered. In 1995 a predominantly African American jury in downtown Los Angeles acquitted O.J. A few years later, Orange County declared bankruptcy.

Athletically, the city experienced a decade-long decline. For the first time the Lakers were mediocre over a period of years. A stray gang bullet grazed a USC football player during practice, and the Trojans dropped well below their historical standards. UCLA won a basketball national championship, but a subsequent scandal resulted in the firing of their coach.

The Dodgers struggled. The Angels blew out the 1995 American League West with one of the most precipitous falls ever.

Much of the shine was gone in the City of the Angels by the late 1990s. In 1999 a resurgence began.

Just as New York City mayor Rudolph Giuliani sparked a reduction in crime, a rise in tourism, and the gentrification of neighborhoods, so too did Mayor Richard Riordan in Los Angeles. Many of those high-tech workers laid off in the wake of cold war victory landed on their feet with the launching of the "Information Superhighway," fueling a big economic comeback.

Shaquille O'Neal, Kobe Bryant, and Phil Jackson led Los Angeles back to the heights of glory. The Anaheim Angels won the 2002 World Series. USC entered into one of the most dominating periods in college football history.

Along with the revival of the city, the Lakers, and L.A. sports in general, one other good thing occurred, or better yet, did not occur. Magic Johnson's HIV never became AIDS.

NUMBERS DON'T LIE
[OR DO THEY?]

33 STRAIGHT!

Until Michael Jordan's 1995–96 Chicago Bulls won 72 regular-season games en route to the title, coach Bill Sharman's 1971–72 Los Angeles Lakers were the elite pro basketball team of all time.

The Lakers set a pro sport consecutive game winning streak of 33 games that remains totally unchallenged to this day. They were 69–13 (the best in league history until the Bulls) and won their first NBA championship.

The mantle "Greatest Team of All Time" is a heady moniker, and in crowning the Lakers it is only fair to mention a few other contenders. Kudos go out to Alex Hannum's 1966–67 Philadelphia 76ers (68–13), the Bill Russell–John Havlicek Boston Celtics teams of the 1960s, and Pat Riley's Showtime Lakers of the 1980s.

Wilt Chamberlain joined up with Jerry West and Elgin Baylor after the 1968 season, but the team's attitude changed significantly when Sharman took over in 1971. The Lakers' problem had never been lack of ability; their problem was too much ability. With ability comes ego, and L.A. was not a big enough town for Baylor and Chamberlain to coexist.

Sharman was a strict disciplinarian, and his early-morning shoot-arounds were anathema to the late-sleeping Wilt (God rest his soul). After Baylor's injuries forced him into an abrupt retirement after a few games, and the team's 4–0 start made the Stilt realize they had a chance to win it all, Chamberlain sacrificed his snooze time for the good of the team.

"I approached Wilt," remembered Sharman, "and he explained that he usually slept until noon, but if it would help the team he'd try it. Once we started winning, Wilt gained confidence that the shootarounds worked."

Baylor's departure with the team at 6–3 placed a heavy load on Jim McMillian and Happy Hairston, but they turned out to be the

Jerry West curls around a pick set by Wilt Chamberlain as the Lakers are on their way to winning the 28th of their NBA record 33 consecutive games in the 1971–1972 season.

STREAKING

151—Concord (California) De La Salle's all-time high school football winning streak, 1992–2004

88—UCLA's all-time college basketball winning streak, 1971–74

47—Oklahoma's all-time college football winning streak, 1953–57

26—New York Giants all-time Major League Baseball winning streak, 1916

21—New England Patriots all-time NFL winning streak, 2003–04

17—Pittsburgh Penguins all-time NHL winning streak, 1992–93

kind of role players Sharman cherished. Ex-Bruin Gail Goodrich hooked up in the backcourt with West, who was still at the height of his game.

Sharman and West both scoffed at the "too much talent" label some placed on the Lakers in the 1960s. "Baylor was one of the all-time greats," Sharman said. "I would have loved to have coached him when he was younger."

West basically felt the Chamberlain-Baylor feud was a myth created by the press. "I don't buy that," he said. "Some styles don't mesh, but the reality is that Elgin had reached a point in his career, as we all do, where with injuries you no longer can compete."

After a brief stumble, magic started to happen at the Forum, and it wasn't named Earvin Johnson. The ultimate luxury arena at the time, it was packed for every game. The Lakers won five straight...nine straight...15 straight...22...27...they just would not lose. Fall passed into winter, and winter was ready to pass into the usual early Southern California spring when Los Angeles took their 33-game winning streak against the Milwaukee Bucks.

That was the year Lew Alcindor changed his name to Kareem Abdul-Jabbar. By the time of the big showdown, Kareem's name was not a mystery, but stopping him was. Abdul-Jabbar made Chamberlain look old, and the Bucks won big. It was only a temporary setback for the Lakers, who cruised to the end, breaking the 76ers' single-season win record by a game. They set a league mark for victory margin over Golden State, 162–99, and scored over the century mark in all but a single contest.

Chicago fell in four straight in the first round of the playoffs, but then came Milwaukee again. In the series opener, Los Angeles collapsed, scoring only 72 points in a game that had everybody convinced that the team would fall apart just like they did at that time every year. Everybody except the players.

"It was a frustrating game," remembered West. "We tried so hard, yet it seemed we couldn't even make a layup. We had such a terrific road team, though, that we had confidence we could beat the Bucks."

Sharman was a calming influence. "I just told them that they had proved themselves to be the best team in the league," he explained. The collapse may have occurred but for McMillian, who was a scoring machine in a desperate back-and-forth death struggle ultimately won by the Lakers, 135–134, to even things out at 1–1. West, Chamberlain, & Co., after catching their breath, began to play the kind of basketball that had gotten them that far in the first place. L.A.'s dominance was ultimately apparent in their 4–2 series win.

Still, Walt Frazier and the New York Knickerbockers stood between Los Angeles and their first championship. The Knicks, who had broken their hearts two years before, ran away with the series opener. Again the skeptics were out in force: "The Lakers

TOP FIVE ALL-TIME SINGLE-SEASON NBA TEAMS

1. 1995–96 Chicago Bulls
2. 1971–72 Los Angeles Lakers
3. 1996–97 Chicago Bulls
4. 1966–67 Philadelphia 76ers
5. 1964–65 Boston Celtics

THAT CHAMPIONSHIP SEASON

Probably the greatest year in the history of California sports was 1972. Aside from the Lakers, championship teams from the Golden State included the Oakland A's (baseball), USC (college football, baseball), and UCLA (college basketball). In addition, Richard Nixon of California won the presidency that year by the largest vote in history (62 percent, 49 states).

don't have heart...the Lakers can't beat an East Coast team." This time the skeptics were wrong. L.A. flattened New York in four straight, winning Game 5 in a runaway before an ecstatic home crowd.

In the jubilant winning clubhouse, West, the superstar denied glory so many times over the years, looked far more relieved than ultimately happy.

"That may be true," Jerry said. "It was enormously frustrating—to the point we felt cursed after all those years. The difference with that team was not only did we feel we could win any game, but we could, to be frank, dominate anybody."

So, Jerry, were the '72 Lakers the greatest team ever assembled?

"You can't compare eras," West answered diplomatically. Many have, and at least until the 1995–96 Bulls, the '72 Lakers were the best ever.

Numbers don't lie. (Or do they?)

CAMELOT AND FIGUEROA

There are very few dynasties in sports history that quite match up to the three-year championship run of the Los Angeles Lakers from 1999 to 2002. There have been other three-time consecutive champions. The Celtics, of course. The Green Bay Packers (1965–67), the New York Yankees (1949–53), the UCLA Bruins (1967–73), the A's of the early '70s; statistically, there have been more impressive runs here and there.

That 1999–2000 team is up there with the 1967 76ers, the 1972 Lakers, the 1996 Bulls, and a few other teams, but in general it would not be regarded as the best of all time. However, the 1999–2000 Lakers not only revived the franchise, they revived the city and the entire National Basketball Association.

The previous year (1998–99) the players, blinded by greed, made the same egregious mistake that baseball and football players had made: they went on strike. America could care less. The resounding sentiment in sports bars and among fans of other sports was, "I hope they stay on strike and don't come back."

The general public had had it up to here with spoiled, over-priced prima donnas, most of whom would have been somewhat helpless if forced to compete in a nonsports environment, demanding not merely that the world owed them a living, but that their entourages and offspring be kept in limo style for a couple of generations to boot.

Basketball was *down*. Baseball had finally recovered from its 1994 strike, although in hindsight the Mark McGwire–Sammy Sosa home run chase of 1998 was someplace between a joke and a hoax. But the Showtime 1980s were a distant memory. Michael was gone. His strange comebacks and the investment in the Washington Wizards were the closest thing to excitement in the NBA.

The league needed marquee players and success in high-profile markets. To say that Shaquille O'Neal, Kobe Bryant, and Phil Jackson saved the NBA would be an exaggeration. To say that without them the league was headed toward a modern version of the 1970s would not be. The likes of Allen Iverson and Rasheed Wallace were not going to revitalize the NBA. Karl Malone, Tim Duncan, David Robinson—all good players, but basketball messiahs they weren't.

THE ZEN MASTER IN SUMMER

Phil Jackson spends off-seasons on a ranch in Montana.

The league breathed a sigh of relief when Shaq came to L.A., when Bryant panned out instead of becoming just another failed high-school-to-the-pros guy, and when Jackson brought his philosophies to Tinseltown. It all worked out so delightfully when STAPLES Center opened and the Lakers baptized it with glory in year one.

The trio of Shaq, Kobe, and Phil created a basketball Renaissance in Los Angeles when they joined forces on the Lakers. Photo courtesy of Getty Images.

176

It was Camelot, right there at the corner of Venice and Figueroa Boulevards. A shining city within a city next to the Harbor Freeway, where a proud franchise, a battered but unbowed old town, and a desperate league found salvation in the new millennium.

Shaq of course came first, but despite his enormous talents, the championships did not immediately follow. Magic had coached the team for a while, and it was almost sad. They were so lethargic that contrasted to his great enthusiasm the team was even less impressive than they otherwise seemed. They were a lost bunch in the mid-1990s. A look back at their record indicates they never sunk to the bottom of the league, but by Lakers standards it was dismal. This was Showtime, where basketball was not a game, it was *joie de vivre*. The team instead looked like they were worn down by modern times, hoping to get the game over with so they could beat the traffic. The pace, the busy schedule of life in Los Angeles, it all seemed to weigh down on them. The game they had grown up with, the game of gym rats, of backyard shooting sessions, of playgrounds and high school cheers, had become a business. *Life* had become a business. The kind of dedication and attention to detail that basketball greatness requires had been replaced by clock-watching, by attention deficit disorder, by the fast pace of the City of the Angels.

This state of affairs was even more pronounced when Magic took over for the last 16 games of the 33–49 1993–94 season. His players were bored, playing out the string. Johnson, however, tried to get them to *respect* the game as he had, although in truth he revered it. He put the team through a series of difficult, training camp–style practices, but to this bunch it just seemed like "college stuff."

For three years (1997–99), Shaq and Kobe had played on teams with good records, but they lacked a missing ingredient. Kobe was a huge experiment, as is any kid signed out of high school, but he was as ballyhooed as any of 'em.

In 1999 when STAPLES opened and the team really needed to take the town by storm in order to make their new palace what it was meant to be, that "missing ingredient" was found.

CELEBRITY CORNER

Rick Fox, who married actress Vanessa Williams, was known affectionately as "Pretty Ricky" by his teammates.

Phil Jackson had a résumé. He had *gravitas*. If he could not do it, nobody could. Unlike some basketball coaches, Jackson had been a good player, but better yet, he was a *winner*. At North Dakota (of all places) he was an All-American under Bill Fitch. He was drafted by the New York Knicks and was a member of two NBA champion teams. In 1969–70 he was injured and unable to play on the team that defeated Los Angeles in a memorable seven-game slugfest. He helped key the 1973 Knicks to victory over L.A. That was a *team*. Jackson learned under Red Holzman the very essence of team play.

After basketball he got into coaching and TV work. He was erudite and intelligent, with a desire for knowledge. He read books and courted ideas on religious philosophy, self-improvement, mind over matter.

In 1989 Jackson was named head coach of the Chicago Bulls. He had at his disposal perhaps the most remarkable player the game has ever known, the great Michael Jordan. For several years coaches had been trying to figure out a way to harness Michael's talents. Jordan had scored the winning basket in North Carolina's 1982 NCAA championship game and then came into the league full of hope for greatness, which he quickly fulfilled.

Jordan would score an ungodly number of points, but the Bulls had never been a great team and Chicago was not a pro basketball town. His scoring totals on teams that did not go all the way looked like selfishness, but Jackson quickly deciphered that Jordan wanted to win more than anybody. He scored because he knew no other way to get his team over the hump. He needed help.

The help came in the form of Jackson's structure, which Phil had the good fortune and intelligence to learn, accept, and adopt from assistant coach Tex Winter. Winter was a holdover Jackson retained on his staff instead of egotistically bringing in his own guys. Tex was *literally* a basketball coach's basketball coach. He had starred and then coached at USC. He had been an institution at Kansas State, coached the San Diego Rockets, and taken over for Jerry Tarkanian at Long Beach State. He told Phil about this offense that could utilize Michael's skills. It was called the "triangle." Tex had learned it under a fellow named Sam Barry, the most legendary USC coach you never heard of.

The rest is history. In short, none did it better. Jackson and Jordan were to basketball what Monet is to impressionism, Heifetz to the violin. Jackson was the kind of coach who would read about a Monet or a Heifetz and find something about their success that he could impart to Jordan, Scottie Pippen, even Dennis Rodman.

The string played itself out, and in 1998 Jackson probably figured he had earned himself a life's vacation in Maui, or at least his version of a vacation, which might very well have been pursuing the study of Plato and Truth at Harvard or someplace. But the man could not resist the chance to mold Shaq and Kobe into the same incredible thing he had in Chicago. The building of STAPLES Center, Jerry Buss's money, and—truth be told—the Hollywood stage, were too alluring. In 1999 he found himself working in downtown Los Angeles.

MEDIA MONSTERS

"But in Los Angeles, unlike Chicago, the agenda is different, more dangerous. In Chicago, the vibe I received from the press was one of adoration for Michael, for the team, everyone reveling in the success we generated for a franchise that until this new era arrived, never hung a championship banner from its rafters. In L.A., which has 14 banners, reporters want to know: what can I write that advances the drama for one more day?"

—Phil Jackson, 2004

The record speaks for itself, of course: 67–15, 56–26, and 58–24 in three NBA championship seasons beginning in 1999 and ending in 2002. He is the first person in NBA history to lead a team to three-straight NBA titles three times. Their 15–1 2001 playoff run is unprecedented. He tied Red Auerbach for the most NBA titles. From 1996 to 2003 he led his teams to an NBA-record 25 consecutive series victories.

Just as a college coach who creates a dynasty in the BCS era or a big-league manager who wins baseball's new multiple playoffs is more impressive than those who did it in the past, Jackson's record of accomplishment is greater than Auerbach's. His teams had to win more playoffs and hurdle greater obstacles to achieve ultimate victory.

THE WRONG SIDE OF THE LAW

HOTEL CALIFORNIA

There is plenty of drama, some sports version of semitragedy, some *actual* tragedy, and maybe a little malice that is *bad* and *ugly*, but the Lakers have been one of the most consistently good franchises in sports history.

But after winning the 1972 NBA title, the Lakers did begin a perilous slide. The very nature of their team changed. An era truly came to an end. While a new one, and eventually a better one, would emerge, it would not be without a *bad* period.

In some ways, the Lakers of 1973–76 represented a morass in which the team's fortunes seemed to mirror those of America's. Of course, 1972 was a big year for the country, the state, the city, and the team. Richard Nixon opened up relations with Red China, brought American involvement in the Vietnam War to its closing days, and won reelection in the greatest landslide ever.

The Lakers did not merely win big; they won in historical fashion, as did two other Los Angeles dynasties, the Southern Cal football team and the UCLA basketball squad.

Entering 1973, there was a sense that great things were on the verge of happening, but as anybody who studies the lessons of history can tell you, this is often the recipe for disaster. No sooner did the POWs return from Vietnam and "peace with honor" was achieved than the nation discovered a place called the Watergate Hotel. Out of that disaster came oil embargoes, an economic

THE UGLY

Cazzie Russell was a collegiate star who enjoyed success in the NBA but never quite lived up to what was expected of him. In 1974–75, he injured his knee and the roof caved in on the 30–52 Lakers (fifth place in the Pacific Division).

downturn, Nixon's resignation, the fall of Saigon, and a sense of post-'60s angst manifesting itself in the form of bad hair, bad clothes, bad music, bad morals, and bad drugs. The latter would characterize the NBA and the Lakers. It would create a major low for the Association—a low that a new Lakers team would help the NBA rise out of. But that was down the road.

After losing to the Knicks in 1973, Wilt Chamberlain left the club, trying to "find" himself through a series of postglory adventures (movies, beach volleyball, sexual records). The 1973–74 Lakers were actually a fairly good team, except that by their standards it was a mediocre season (47–35, still first in the Pacific Division). Gail Goodrich scored 25.3 points a game. Jerry West averaged 20.3 but was injured for 51 games. He called it quits after the team fell in the playoffs. In 1974, it seemed as if fate were playing a joke on Los Angeles. Boston won the NBA title.

Boston. Again.

But 1974–75 was a new low, perhaps an all-time low. The Lakers fell to fifth in the Pacific Division (30–52). Poor Bill Sharman, who could barely talk, presided over the mess of the season. The consummate professional, with his attention to detail and hard-charging daily style, now all his methods looked foolish. Sharman was a man who approached each day at work the same, whether the team was 69–13 or 30–52, but if he expected that he could get pro basketball players on a losing team to be that professional, he was sadly mistaken.

On top of all that, the 1975 NBA champions were the Golden State Warriors, longtime Lakers doormats. They were a team that always thought the Lakers were their rivals, but over the years the

Lakers hardly gave them a second thought. They rode into San Francisco and Oakland, dispatched the Warriors like the Roman legion quelling a territorial uprising, and then moved on.

The Lakers fans proved something during these years that has pretty well held for decades. They are front-runners. The Los Angeles fan is, with only two exceptions, a front-runner. To the extent that the Los Angeleno is loyal, that loyalty has been granted to only two teams through thick and thin: the Trojans and the Dodgers. The Lakers, Angels, Kings, Ducks, Raiders, Rams, Bruins—they get their props when they win, which is often enough, but are forgotten like yesterday's news when they do not.

Only a few years earlier, the "Fabulous Forum" was all that, the biggest party this side of Oscar night. But when the team slid and their marquee stars either retired or got long in the tooth, the Hollywood hotties and Beverly Hills power brokers disappeared, finding new "best friends" at Dodger Stadium or the Coliseum.

However, a core of "true believers" would emerge. Many of those who are most loyal to the team have not necessarily been season ticket holders, especially as prices escalated over the years. But through Chick Hearn's radio voice and KCAL's TV broadcasts, then eventually with the escalation of sports-talk radio, blue-collar Lakers supporters have stayed with the team.

The 1960s had been a vibrant, albeit perhaps misguided, period in American history. Regardless of what one's politics were, there was no denying that the protesting youth were energized

THE BAD

The low point of the 1974–75 campaign came when the Lakers went on a six-game losing streak, beginning with a 109–87 thumping at Seattle on February 16 and concluding with an overtime defeat against the Trail Blazers on February 26. Included in the streak was a 12-point defeat at the hands of eventual NBA champion Golden State.

The Lakers and Kareem would have their headaches in the mid-1970s as the team, fans, and indeed the nation at large hit the doldrums emblematic of the era.

and idealistic. But out of that grew the long hair, the hippie styles, the music scene, and of course the drugs.

By the festering mid-1970s, all that was really left was a drug *culture*. There was no real political movement anymore. Nixon had been ousted and the war was over. Pundits stopped talking about the cold war. Kids tried to stylize their long hair, but it looked worse than it did when it just grew naturally. They wore disco shirts and flared pants with high-heeled boots. Observers of old footage automatically laugh at the ridiculousness of it. The music became commercialized.

All of this had a major effect on sports. Kids lacked discipline. They partied and took drugs in the eighth grade. An old-school

Bill Sharman/Jerry West type of guy was mocked. The Lakers were as affected by this as any team. Los Angeles became a disco scene, and the Lakers took it in, partying at the clubs that sprouted up: Flanagan's in Marina del Rey, the Red Onion in Redondo Beach.

Lakers management was forced to employ off-duty L.A. police detectives—known as "narcs" within the drug culture—to identify drugs and hookers, two interchangeable things. The sexual revolution was full blown in this pre-AIDS era. New racial sensibilities had removed the last vestiges of white-black taboo. The Lakers partook of all manner of sensory pleasures, with little good result on the basketball court. Sharman did not have the foggiest idea how to relate to any of it. Wilt Chamberlain's peccadilloes seemed innocent and far off.

Security consultants regularly provided surveillance reports of drug activity. The players were infuriated that they were being spied on, as if their employers did not have the slightest right to expect that the men to whom they paid escalating salaries should actually come to work in good health, prepared to perform at peak levels.

At first the problem had been marijuana, which infuriated the old school but was thought to be relatively harmless. It did not cause weight gain, and some even felt it relaxed players, allowing them to play better. But it is a gateway drug, and it escalated to cocaine, which is a dangerous, addictive, life-destroying substance.

SOCIAL PROGRESS

"Wilt was a powerful black man, a symbol to an entire race; there was no way he should have denigrated his people, particularly in front of a white public guaranteed to seize upon this racist assertion as another means to divide and control us. Wilt had gone too far. I stopped seeing him as a political crossover and began to think of him as a traitor."

Kareem Abdul-Jabbar, 1983, commenting on Chamberlain's assertions about black female sexuality

Coke had been around a long time. Coca-Cola—"the real thing"—was actually made with cocaine until around 1904, with athletes endorsing it for "pepping" them up. *Sherlock Holmes* author Sir Arthur Conan Doyle allegedly wrote while on cocaine. But it escalated in the 1960s. At first it was a "Hollywood drug," but by the mid-1970s it had made its way to New York and then mainstream America.

By 1975 the kinds of debilitating, life-threatening, and sometimes even life-ending results of habitual cocaine use were not widely understood. What was even worse than snorting it, however, was a new rage: "freebasing," or in showbiz party circles, "playing baseball." Hollywood's favorite team, the Los Angeles Lakers, were now Tinseltown's favorite party invitees. The predominantly white movie crowd loved feeling good about themselves by inviting black athletes. Jim Brown and Wilt Chamberlain made the scene, to say the least. Hugh Hefner, having moved from chilly Chicago to Los Angeles, threw outrageous parties at his Holmby Hills mansion on Charing Cross Road off of Sunset. Like the song says, it was the "Hotel California." Many who "checked in" could "never leave," at least not without paying "heavenly bills."

"You worried like hell," recalled Pete Newell, who replaced Fred Schaus as the Lakers' general manager in 1972.

"Marijuana and drugs always seemed to break out at parties. The players were celebrities, so they were always invited. And they were anxious to meet the people they saw in the movies. A lot of Hollywood power people liked to showcase the athletes."

BUSINESS COMES FIRST

After Kermit Washington punched out Rudy Tomjanovich in 1978, he, Don Chaney, and a first-round draft pick were traded to Boston for Charlie Scott. With no rebounding help, Kareem Abdul-Jabbar was all alone. The team floundered until Magic Johnson got there.

However, "We didn't really test the players for drugs because cocaine was not something that was feared that much back then," Newell reasoned.

Everybody dressed like a drug dealer in those days, so identifying who was selling to the players was no easy task. They were glorified on TV shows. To be "clean" was to be square. Anybody could be holding, selling, using. It was perhaps even worse on the road, where there were no constraints from wives, children, and family. Crowds of people met the team in hotel lobbies bearing drugs like gifts for visiting potentates. The smell of pot was so pungent in Oakland that Newell could not sleep, and "the place was wall-to-wall hookers."

The hookers were especially troubling, because they were not "traditional" prostitutes offering sex for money. NBA players had enough women available to them for free without paying for it anyway. But this new breed of party girl wanted cocaine and was happy to trade sexual favors for it. The physical act was not the thing anymore; it was the drug. Sex was just part of the sensation that went with the whole soul-destroying act.

The whole scene appalled Cooke, Newell, and the so-called moralists.

The women "just flaunted themselves," said Newell, who added, "There was no deterrence about AIDS and sex in those days."

But the players' moral and physical well-being was not the only casualty of the 1970s. The average fan was still an upscale white male. They knew what was going on and had little sympathy or interest in these players. They voted with their pocketbooks, and as a result attendance and TV ratings sank in the years following the great Lakers-Celtics and Lakers-Knicks matchups.

After the retirements of Russell, Baylor, West, and Chamberlain, the NBA's marquee player was Kareem Abdul-Jabbar, who came to Los Angeles in 1975 after six years in Milwaukee. Abdul-Jabbar wrote a long article for *Sports Illustrated* after he got out of UCLA that did little for his public image. In that piece, Abdul-Jabbar informed the world that he had rejected Christianity in favor of Islam, which went over like a dead weight. He also freely admitted to having experimented with cocaine and heroin in college. He expressed admiration for John Wooden but said that as a white man of a certain age, it was impossible for Wooden to understand what he went through as a young black man.

Abdul-Jabbar was one of the greatest athletes of all time. He has many supporters to this day who argue that he, not Michael Jordan or anybody else, is the finest basketball player who ever lived. The numbers, the championships, the college and high school years, the longevity—when added all up it is a compelling argument. Despite that, at the very height of his fame and powers, he was not a very popular player. Abdul-Jabbar was taciturn, he always seemed to have a grievance, and fans had no empathy for his complaints.

In Abdul-Jabbar's first year with the Lakers (1975–76), the club went 40–42 under Bill Sharman. Abdul-Jabbar averaged almost 28 points a game and earned MVP honors. Goodrich scored 19.5, and Abdul-Jabbar's UCLA teammate, Lucius Allen, scored just shy of 15. Cazzie Russell, a star at Michigan a decade earlier whose career had been beset by injuries, scored 11.8.

During the period following the 1972 title, nothing ever seemed to run smoothly. Chamberlain's retirement came at a time in which the team was unable to make immediate arrangements for a replacement, which led to the loss of Jim McMillian. Cooke took the better part of a year out of town righting the ship of one of his other companies. Sharman also spent most of the 1973–74 season in New York, where his wife was hospitalized with the cancer that eventually killed her.

West's departure, which should have been a glory road, was acrimonious—"The worst time of my life," he said. In the mid-1960s, West arranged with Cooke that he would always be paid more than Elgin Baylor "because he did so much more," said Cooke. But Chamberlain made more. West believed that Cooke had made the same promise to Chamberlain. Cooke denied it, and out of that bad feelings emerged.

"Jerry West was a brilliant young man in many areas," Cooke said. "But he was very naïve back then in the ways of the world. Jerry was obsessed with money. He's a very rich man now. He's been very careful in the handling of his money."

WANNA BET?

The league was "floundering," Jerry West said of the period after his retirement. Aside from drugs, gambling was a problem, too. The nature of the NBA schedule, teams falling out of contention, wide swings in scores, and of course "garbage time" at the end of games made pro basketball a target for bettors. A basketball player can affect the spread better than any other athlete, except perhaps the baseball pitcher, who only gets a start every fifth game and is not likely to "throw" those precious outings. The Lakers had to expand their detective force from the dressing room and Forum vicinity to the Hollywood beat, where the drug and betting connections were free to happen.

West said he did not have a problem with a player making more than he did, but rather the manner of Cooke's manipulation of salary talk by pitting players against each other.

"No one ever had to pay me to play basketball," said West, but the negotiations were "acrimonious" because it was "a game to him."

Drugs plagued the league until the 1980s. In 1986 Len Bias, having just been drafted second overall by Boston, died of an acute cardiac arrhythmia in his dorm room after snorting too much cocaine at an off-campus party.

In 1982 Commissioner David Stern finally instituted a drug policy with some bite to it. Society began to tolerate drug use less and less. Whether AIDS put a true damper on the players' amorous adventures, however, is another story.

THE PUNCH

Early in the 1977–78 season, Kareem Abdul-Jabbar was battling for position with Milwaukee rookie Kent Benson when Benson shot a forearm into Kareem's solar plexus. Abdul-Jabbar knocked Benson unconscious with a single Bill Sharman–style punch. The impact broke Kareem's hand and he was out for 20 games.

Power forward Kermit Washington returned from a knee injury and found himself forced to handle the boards alone. Washington, like Sharman, had the reputation of being a sweet, gentle family man. Also like Sharman, he was ultracompetitive on the floor. The 6'8" Washington had come to L.A. from American International University, after having been scouted by Pete Newell. A great rebounder, he was quick and strong. However, he lacked an understanding of the game and was often confused trying to adjust to NBA offensive and defensive strategy.

When Newell took Washington under his wing, it was the nexus for his "Big Man Campuses," which became a staple of development for centers and power forwards over the years. Had he played for Los Angeles a few years earlier, he would not have had the chance to improve his skills. The great Lakers of that era wouldn't have wasted their efforts developing a player who was not ready for the big time. But he played during a period in which the team was down. Newell made him a "project."

"Kermit is a special person to me," said Newell.

Washington became protective of Abdul-Jabbar. One night he got so physical with Boston's Dave Cowens that the Celtics center punched him in the face. It did not faze Washington. Washington just backhanded him. When Kevin Stacom entered the fray, Kermit smacked him in the nose. Don Nelson confronted Washington but decided discretion was the better part of valor. He backed off.

Washington got into it with the Buffalo Braves, too. He told Newell that he was gun-shy about getting hit from behind, which was becoming common. It reminded him of the fear he had felt growing up in the inner city, where gang fights broke out all the time.

"He told me that in the ghetto you always made sure there was a wall at your back when you got into hassles," Newell recalled.

In December the Houston Rockets visited the Forum. Washington grabbed Kevin Kunnert's shorts to hold him back, not an uncommon form of gamesmanship. Kunnert swung at Washington, but Abdul-Jabbar broke it up. At that point, Rockets star Rudy Tomjanovich raced up to help his teammate.

Sensing Tomjanovich from behind, Washington reeled and threw a punch that landed square, sounding to courtside observers like a "melon" hitting pavement. The combination of Tomjanovich's momentum, Kermit's karate-quick punch, and perfect timing resulted in one of the worst punches in NBA history. Tomjanovich went down in a heap, blood everywhere. It was reminiscent of the brutal beating administered by Minnesota players to Ohio State's Luke Witte in a 1972 Big Ten game.

The blow was replayed constantly on television. Washington received hate mail. The incident had a terrible effect on Washington and his family. Tomjanovich never truly recovered

Rudy Tomjanovich was still wearing a bulky protective mask the season *after* Kermit Washington caved in his face with a brutal punch on the court.

WINNERS

Lou Hudson was a perennial all-star with the Atlanta Hawks who came to the Lakers toward the end of his career. He played in L.A. from 1977 to 1979, averaging 13.7 points in his first year.

his all-star status, although he did lead the Rockets to consecutive NBA titles as a coach in 1994–95.

Washington was fined $50,000 and suspended 60 days without pay. Tomjanovich sued and won. Race reared its ugly head, of course, with Washington's black teammates claiming that had Washington been white the incident would have been forgotten.

Cooke and the team did not support Washington in his civil trial, and he was traded. It was in many ways the final straw for Cooke and the Lakers. The attitude worked both ways. Cooke went through the costliest divorce in recorded history. His ex-wife, Jeannie, had attempted suicide four times. Cooke once had broken his own arm in an effort to prevent her from leaving him at their Sierra Nevada vacation home.

Jeannie was awarded $41 million, judged at the time by the *Guinness Book of World Records* to be the biggest settlement in history. In order to meet the payment, Cooke was forced to sell his Forum sports empire, which in turn set another record.

Jack Kent Cooke had built the Lakers and the Forum. He brought hockey to L.A. and presided over greatness. His contributions were many and worthy of tremendous admiration, but he had a reputation as a tyrant who lacked people skills. His departure from the scene left little sadness. Jerry West, for one, was elated.

TARK AND THE MURDER MYSTERY

In 1976 Jack Kent Cooke wanted to hire UNLV's Jerry Tarkanian as the Lakers coach. When Nevada–Las Vegas boosters got wind of it, they raised such a stink that it fell through. Cooke was "forced" to hire Jerry West. Their acrimonious relationship never really improved.

In the spring of 1979, the Lakers were on the verge of a new era. Magic Johnson was drafted as a result of good luck. The Lakers had traded an over-the-hill Gail Goodrich to the New Orleans Jazz in a convoluted deal that threatened to involve the commissioner's office. In the end, that deal led to the Lakers and the Chicago Bulls engaging in a coin flip to determine who would get the rights to draft Magic Johnson number one. Everything worked out for Los Angeles. Johnson was a sophomore. For years, the NBA could only draft a player whose senior class had graduated. "Hardship" court cases eliminated those rules, which was how Johnson was eligible. In fact, the "father" of NBA hardship cases, Spencer Haywood, would be Magic's teammate in 1979–80.

Many skeptics have said the coin flip that gave the Johnson draft pick to L.A. was rigged so the superstar went to Los Angeles. Certainly the confluence of Johnson in L.A. and Bird in Boston did seem almost too good to be true.

Also that spring, Cooke was finalizing his sale of the team to Jerry Buss. Aside from this, the team needed a new coach. They went after Tarkanian in earnest, and now "Tark the Shark" wanted the job for real.

Buss asked Cooke to arrange a meeting with Tarkanian. Cooke quickly phoned Tarkanian, whose number he kept handy. Tarkanian was in New York City recruiting Sidney Green. A meeting was agreed to, but a vow of silence was promised so as to avoid the same kind of leak as had happened three years earlier.

After a meeting in California, Buss called in his agent and good friend, Vic Weiss, to work out the details. Weiss was a 51-year-old San Fernando Valley auto dealer and boxing manager who arrived at the meeting in a white Rolls.

He met with Buss and Cooke. In the course of that conversation Weiss pulled out a wad of cash, about $5,000 or $10,000. It was a *Goodfellas* move, although its effect on two legitimate businessmen, Cooke and Buss, negotiating for a legitimate basketball coach, was negligible, as in, "What's he trying to prove?"

VOICES

Stu Lantz played in L.A. only from 1974 to 1976 and was never a star on great teams, but he is a well-known Laker. He broadcasted their games for over 20 years, mostly as Chick Hearn's color man.

Eventually a contract was agreed to: five years for $1 million. The meeting went late, and it was agreed they would finish some minor details about Tarkanian's ticket allotments and company cars the next day.

Tarkanian was supposed to arrive for that meeting after Weiss and the "two owners" had hammered out the ticket and car arrangements, at which time an announcement could be made and the contract signed. Cooke and Buss arrived, but Weiss did not. They called Tarkanian at his Newport Beach hotel room. He had not heard from Weiss. Then Weiss's wife phoned Tarkanian to say he had not come home the night before. The meeting was called off.

Days passed without word from Weiss. In the meantime, the contract was put on hold. Then a parking attendant at the Universal Sheraton noticed a foul odor. It was Weiss, stuffed into the trunk of a car. He was still carrying a rough draft of Tarkanian's contract.

Weiss was involved in "shady deals with Rams owner Carroll Rosenbloom," said Tarkanian. "I heard he was transporting money for Rosenbloom."

The plot thickened. Rosenbloom had long been suspected of high-stakes gambling and underworld connections. Just a few weeks earlier Rosenbloom had drowned in Florida in what was probably murder.

Federal authorities had linked Weiss to Rosenbloom and were investigating his role in transporting cash to Las Vegas in order to place bets for the Rams owner. A surveillance tape showed Weiss exchanging a briefcase in a Vegas restroom, but there was not enough evidence to connect all the dots. The whole lurid story

Jerry Tarkanian was the front-runner to be the Lakers next coach in 1979 until a murder mystery derailed his chances. Photo courtesy of Getty Images.

had the unfortunate effect of linking Tarkanian to organized crime. This was an easy enough connection for people to make about a coach in Las Vegas. He was already notorious for breaking NCAA recruiting violations, not to mention bringing in recruits who often had criminal backgrounds.

The L.A.P.D. spent years on the case. It was never solved but was assumed to be a hit. Its effect on the Lakers was that news reports of the killing tipped UNLV backers that Tarkanian was again planning to take the L.A. job. They put a guilt trip on Tark. He turned down a chance to coach Magic Johnson, Kareem Abdul-Jabbar, and the Showtime Lakers in his hometown of Los Angeles.

"Going in with Magic would have been something," he said.

SCANDAL

"I CRIED WHEN I FOUND OUT."

"He's got something," said Michael Ovitz, at one time considered the most powerful man in Hollywood, of Earvin "Magic" Johnson. "He's a star among stars."

Indeed, Magic Johnson was a megastar in a town of superstars. It has often been said that, aside from select political figures, war heroes, and maybe a few astronauts, there is no greater height to ascend to than the New York sports icon.

Marilyn Monroe, who was as big as they come, discovered this when she returned from a tour of Korea.

"Joe, Joe," she exclaimed to her husband, ex-Yankees great Joe DiMaggio, "you never *heard* such cheering."

DiMaggio, who was as cold as a dead fish, just looked at her and said, "Yes, I have."

DiMaggio and a handful of others have ascended to the heights of iconography in the Big Apple, but Los Angeles is just as big a stage, in many ways even larger. Surrounded by Hollywood glitz and glamour, most athletes pale in comparison, but a handful rise above all of them.

Kareem Abdul-Jabbar, possibly the greatest basketball player who ever lived, never came close. Wilt Chamberlain was larger than life, but his career highlights were in Philadelphia, his L.A. years marred by as much disappointment as glory. Jerry West was

IT AIN'T OVER TILL IT'S OVER

Magic Johnson returned to play effectively in 32 games for the Lakers in 1995–96.

almost a tragic figure. Sandy Koufax's star shone brightly, but he was a recluse.

Magic was the ultimate athlete-celebrity. He was also the ultimate athlete–sex symbol. He would charge up the crowds, but looking at them watching him—Jack Nicholson, Spike Lee, Paula Abdul, Arsenio Hall, Eddie Murphy, Rob Lowe, Charlie Sheen, Denzel Washington, Lou Gossett Jr., Janet Jackson, Don Johnson, Lionel Ritchie, Whitney Houston—they would sit in those front-row seats watching Magic in awe, and it jazzed him up even more.

The athlete, particularly the basketball player performing in the intimate court setting, can connect with fans like few others. Magic did it like none before or since. Unlike the movie star, performing take after take in front of camera and crew but minus audience participation, the athlete has the immediate gratification of the crowd.

Magic's balletic performances in front of genuflecting movie stars, hot starlets, and sexy Laker Girls had a seductive quality to them. He seemed to be "strutting his stuff" like a peacock performing a mating dance, and the ladies came flocking. Magic was huge everywhere. He was big in Europe, in Asia, in Latin America...

"After every game, we'd have this entourage, this line of cars behind our team bus, that would follow us to the airport in hopes of getting a glimpse of Earvin..." said Lakers broadcaster Stu Lantz.

Norm Nixon was the Lakers' resident playboy when Magic arrived. He showed the rookie the ropes, but it was not long before Johnson was "the Man." His teammates, of course, followed him like a pied piper. Only the top rock stars or movie actors ever had such a life. Girls constantly approached teammates.

"Where's Magic? Can you give Magic my phone number?"

Johnson later stated that he had sex with so many women not just to satiate his own desires but to *accommodate* them, almost out of a sense of egalitarian fairness.

"It has been said that Los Angeles became Magic's city," wrote Roland Lazenby in *The Lakers: A Basketball Journey*. "More accurately, it became his harem."

Chamberlain claimed twenty thousand, but Magic was on pace to erase that statistic from the record books. Magic claimed, "three hundred to five hundred women annually."

Magic found them at the Forum, at nightclubs, at the gym, at the beach. It was L.A. No place compares to L.A. when it comes to beautiful, available, single women.

"They want the thrill of being with an athlete," explained Dominique Wilkins of the Atlanta Hawks in *Sports Illustrated*. "And they don't want safe sex. They want to have your baby, man, because they think that if they have your baby, they're set for life. That's the hard fact of it, because if they had a life, they wouldn't be hanging around the hotel or showing up at the back door of the arena trying to pick up a player."

The athletes encouraged that behavior. There was little discretion among the Lakers, just bragging, boasting, "note sharing," even statistics keeping. Jerry Buss did not just encourage it, he participated in it, although he later said, "I didn't realize there was as much activity as there was." Pat Riley had no control over it.

Johnson had one rule, however. He always kicked the girl(s) out before daybreak. He had a girlfriend back in East Lansing named Earleatha "Cookie" Kelly, whom he had known since high school. Incredibly, she stayed with him through all of this but did not move to L.A. Magic saw her in the off-seasons.

COMEBACK

Magic Johnson was elected to the Hall of Fame in 2002. It completed a remarkable comeback from the HIV announcement of 1991.

In 1981 a "gay disease" reared its ugly head in San Francisco. It spread through the homosexual bathhouses of The Castro, Greenwich Village, and West Hollywood, then throughout the country. It was called HIV, which always eventually became AIDS. Lakers trainer Gary Vitti knew about it. The word was that it was strictly a homosexual disease, but Vitti worried about it anyway. He started handing out condoms to Lakers players, but many disdained them.

A meeting was held in Hawaii in which the subject of sexually transmitted diseases and AIDS came up. One member of the Lakers laughed and said that "if Magic Johnson did not have it, you can't get it."

That line became a catchphrase, a joke in Lakers circles.

In August of 1991, Johnson proposed to Cookie. A prenuptial agreement was signed, protecting Magic's $100 million, followed by a quick wedding before training camp started. Magic then went to camp. Before the season began the Lakers jetted to Paris for an exhibition tour. It was there that Cookie learned she was pregnant. The team returned and went on a whirlwind road trip that included trips to Canada and Utah. On October 25, Johnson got a message from Lon Rosen, his agent, stating he had to return to Los Angeles immediately.

Gary Vitti thought Magic was making an excuse to avoid the end-of-the-training-camp road schedule, so he called the Lakers team doctor, Michael Mellman. Dr. Mellman told him he could not say what the problem was yet, only that something abnormal had shown up on Magic's blood test.

Due to league salary-cap rules, Magic's contract was no longer the biggest in the NBA. In an effort to keep him paid at the top level while circumventing the cap, Jerry Buss arranged a low-interest loan. In order to finalize the loan, Magic needed a life insurance policy. In order to get that, he needed a physical. Now the results were in.

In short order, Magic's mysterious health ailment made its way around Lakers circles, and then became the subject of various rumors throughout the league, the media, and eventually the general public. Nobody knew what was going on, but like a light

Magic announces his retirement from the NBA after learning that he had tested positive for the AIDS virus on November 7, 1991.

going on in his head, Vitti realized in the middle of a game what it was.

He's HIV-positive.

It was assumed by 1991 that AIDS, which starts out as HIV before it becomes full-blown AIDS, could be contracted by males having sexual relations with women. Nobody did more of that than Magic. The next day, Dr. Mellman called. Vitti told him it was HIV before Mellman could tell him.

"I knew you would figure it out," the doctor said.

There was a period of time in which the secret was kept. Slowly but surely everybody on the Lakers team began to suspect that it was HIV. Rumors were rampant. Finally, in a press conference with

WHEN THE FAT LADY SINGS

Magic Johnson played in the 1992 All-Star Game as preparation for the Barcelona Olympic Games.

a live national feed on November 7, 1991, Magic announced to the world that he was HIV-positive.

It was a terrible shock.

"I cried when I found out," said Larry Bird, who had by then befriended Magic.

The news sent shock waves through more than just the media and the public. Thousands of women had had sex with Magic. Then there were all the men who had had sex with those thousands of women. Magic's recent marriage and his wife's pregnancy added to the Shakespearean tragedy of it all. Since that time, however, the entire episode is seen with a new perspective.

First, Magic detected it early, a key to stemming the disease. He fought it the way he took to his basketball career. It was a challenge to be overcome. He and Cookie stayed married. Their child was born without the disease. Cookie has never come down with HIV.

Magic—always in good shape anyway—became a health nut, eating well, working out regularly, and taking steroids for strength in order to combat the HIV. He became a successful businessman with entrepreneurial ventures all over Los Angeles.

In 1992 he participated in the Barcelona Olympics as a member of America's "Dream Team." He later coached the Lakers, although it was during a down period. He became a top Lakers executive.

Medical science has made huge breakthroughs on AIDS research. A man of Magic's wealth can afford the best treatment. His HIV has been held in check and never became AIDS. The disease is not yet curable, but some 16 years after discovering he was HIV-positive, Johnson, while not cured, is a healthy man. He has come to the point where he thinks about the future without concluding that death by AIDS is his only destiny.

Johnson's HIV saga shed new light on AIDS. In the early 1980s it was believed that only homosexual men could contract AIDS. Then women started to get it from their male partners. Pregnant women passed it on to their babies, who were born with it. By the early 1990s it was considered an article of faith that HIV could be contracted by straight men having heterosexual sex. Anybody could get it through a tainted blood transfusion, as happened with tennis star Arthur Ashe. Drug users contracted it by sharing dirty needles.

As for Magic, he may just beat HIV. It would be a wonderful victory, and in the end it could even overshadow his accomplishments on the basketball court.

CELEBRITY CORNER

YOU DON'T KNOW JACK

In Los Angeles, celebrities and sports go together like peanut butter and jelly. In the 1920s and '30s, when USC football coach Howard Jones presided over his legendary four-time national champion "Thundering Herd" Trojans, silent-film stars of the era were regulars at the Coliseum. Gary Cooper and others wrote letters to Jones, asking questions about strategy.

UCLA and Rams quarterback Bob Waterfield got as much attention for his girlfriend, bombshell actress Jane Russell, as he did for his great skills. In the 1960s, Angels playboy lefty Bo Belinsky was the most publicized player in the game, not because he was much on the mound but because his love life included trysts with Mamie Van Doren, Tina Louise, and *Playboy* Playmate of the Year Jo Collins.

When the Dodgers came to town they were an immediate hit. Danny Kaye, Walter Matthau, Doris Day, Cary Grant, and countless others were regulars at Dodger Stadium.

But no team in Hollywood is more associated with Hollywood than the Los Angeles Lakers. Beautiful actresses and models could dress in their best finery without regard to weather conditions at their games. But from the time the Forum was built, the Lakers' Hollywood connection was symbolized by legendary actor Jack Nicholson.

Jack Nicholson, shown here at a 1977 game at the Forum, has been a court-side fixture at Lakers games for decades.

One of the biggest stars of all time, Nicholson hit the scene as the drunken lawyer in *Easy Rider*. Starting with that movie, his reputation was as something of a rebel, a '60s kind of guy. He has never lost that quirky image.

In 1974 he starred in the classic *Chinatown*, one of the greatest movies ever made about Los Angeles. His credits are too numerous to list, but his performance as Col. Nathan Jessep in *A Few Good Men*, opposite Tom Cruise, was *bravura*.

Nicholson just *loves* basketball. A glimpse of this is seen in his 1976 hit *One Flew Over the Cuckoo's Nest*, when he tries to get the recalcitrant, towering Indian "Chief" to dunk a basketball, and in so doing sparks the idea for an escape from the mental hospital.

Nicholson became a fixture on the floor of Lakers games. Jack Kent Cooke ruffled feathers by promoting this. Traditionally,

RIVALRIES

"I had to educate my players who the Celtics were. One day in practice, I asked if anyone knew. Finally Kareem raised his hand. He said the Celtics were a warring race of Danes who invaded Ireland. I had to explain that they were also a cunning, secretive race."

—Pat Riley

those seats were reserved for the press, who sat at a long table. Cooke was unimpressed by the scruffy writers with their beards, unkempt hair, and lack of respect. He moved them to a press area up in the stands, replacing the table with comfortable seats for high-profile Hollywood types to see and be seen.

More often than not, beautiful girls were strategically placed in these seats, causing distraction for fans, writers, players, and cameras. Over the years the scene has gotten out of hand. When the Lakers moved to STAPLES Center in 1999, the battle for front-row seats became a symbol of Hollywood power.

Aside from Nicholson, longtime actress Dyan Cannon has been a regular at Lakers games for decades. She and Jack have remained faithful fans regardless of record in a notoriously front-runner's city. Other regulars included Whoopi Goldberg, John McEnroe, Johnny Carson, and Henry Winkler.

In Game 4 of the 1987 Finals at the Boston Garden, Nicholson managed to get a seat in the upper press area. Boston fans gave him the choke sign.

"There was one guy," Nicholson said, "he was giving me the choke sign so hard, I almost sent for the paramedics. He was wearing a gray sweatshirt, and his face turned almost as gray as his shirt. I couldn't believe it."

Then Nicholson mooned his tormentors.

"I was surprised he didn't get arrested," said equipment manager Rudy Garciduenas. "But the Boston fans loved him being there. He gave them somebody to jeer at."

L.A. won by a point.

Many movies have been filmed at the Forum and STAPLES Center, too. In recent years this included a scene from the HBO series *Entourage*. Perhaps the greatest interaction between basketball and film occurred when *Curb Your Enthusiasm*'s Larry David filmed a scene in which he accidentally trips Shaquille O'Neal, causing the big man a serious injury that makes David a pariah in Los Angeles.

A subsequent scene shows Larry visiting O'Neal, who has acted with some critical acclaim (he was great in *Blue Chips*), in the hospital, where it is determined that—to Larry's relief—Shaq's injury is not serious and he will return to the team quickly.

NOTES

IN THE CLUTCH
Mr. Clutch
"He was almost a perfect person...": Grabowski, John. *The Los Angeles Lakers* (San Diego: Lucent Books, 2002).

ORIGINS
Land of 10,000 Lakes
"It didn't help the smaller guy...": Grabowski, John. *The Los Angeles Lakers* (San Diego: Lucent Books, 2002).

The Triangle
"Barry picked it up from Doc Meanwell when he was a graduate student at Wisconsin...": Travers, Steven. "Glory Days," *StreetZebra*, February 2000.

VOICES
"Hot Rod" Remembers the Lakers' First Year
"I hung out with Bo Belinsky and Dean Chance...": Travers, Steven. "'Hot Rod' Remembers Lakers' First Year," *StreetZebra*, February 2000.

Chickie Baby
"Chick was not one to hold a grudge...": *2006–07 Lakers Media Guide*, 2006.

WHEN THE FAT LADY SINGS
Frustration
"The more I thought about it, the more determined...": Lazenby, Roland. *The Lakers: A Basketball Journey* (New York: St. Martin's Press, 1993).

"It was very, very difficult...": Lazenby, Roland. *The Lakers: A Basketball Journey* (New York: St. Martin's Press, 1993).

"That second half of the season, the team realized...": Lazenby, Roland. *The Lakers: A Basketball Journey* (New York: St. Martin's Press, 1993).

"Born 50 or 100 years earlier, most of the tall...": Chamberlain, Wilt. *A View from Above* (New York: Villard Books, 1991).

Take a Bite Out of the Big Apple
"There's been so much unhappiness connected to my basketball...": Lazenby, Roland. *The Lakers: A Basketball Journey* (New York: St. Martin's Press, 1993).

DADDY DEAREST
The Royal Canadian
"He was the number one asshole who ever lived...": Lazenby, Roland. *The Lakers: A Basketball Journey* (New York: St. Martin's Press, 1993).

"Everybody was on eggshells...": Lazenby, Roland. *The Lakers: A Basketball Journey* (New York: St. Martin's Press, 1993).

"Mr. Cooke shouted and screamed...": Lazenby, Roland. *The Lakers: A Basketball Journey* (New York: St. Martin's Press, 1993).

"That would be nice...": Lazenby, Roland. *The Lakers: A Basketball Journey* (New York: St. Martin's Press, 1993).

Notes

"...on call 24 hours a day, because Jack was on call 24 hours a day...": Lazenby, Roland. *The Lakers: A Basketball Journey* (New York: St. Martin's Press, 1993).

Then Came Sharman
"Egads, they were prima donnas...": Lazenby, Roland. *The Lakers: A Basketball Journey* (New York: St. Martin's Press, 1993).
"We had a lot of players who'd had a lot of personal success...": Lazenby, Roland. *The Lakers: A Basketball Journey* (New York: St. Martin's Press, 1993).
"Whenever he wanted something derogatory...": Lazenby, Roland. *The Lakers: A Basketball Journey* (New York: St. Martin's Press, 1993).

The Player
"There were times when I felt I'd gotten...": Lazenby, Roland. *The Lakers: A Basketball Journey* (New York: St. Martin's Press, 1993).

STADIUM STORIES
The Forum
"Har, har, har...": Lazenby, Roland. *The Lakers: A Basketball Journey* (New York: St. Martin's Press, 1993).
"Two thousand years and six thousand miles east of here...": Lazenby, Roland. *The Lakers: A Basketball Journey* (New York: St. Martin's Press, 1993).

THE GOOD, THE BAD, AND THE UGLY
Just Like Any Other Seven-Foot Black Millionaire Who Lives Next Door
"I really feel I am one of the most misunderstood celebrities...": Chamberlain, Wilt. *A View from Above* (New York: Villard Books, 1991).

"He didn't give him the offensive position...": Lazenby, Roland. *The Lakers: A Basketball Journey* (New York: St. Martin's Press, 1993).

"For so long, all the attention, even the praise...": Abdul-Jabbar, Kareem and Mignon McCarthy. *Kareem* (New York: Random House, 1990).

The Enigma

"I used to get my ass handed to me...": Abdul-Jabbar, Kareem and Peter Knobler. *Giant Steps: The Autobiography of Kareem Abdul-Jabbar* (New York: Bantam Books, 1983).

"Most big boys are awkward...": Grabowski, John. *The Los Angeles Lakers* (San Diego: Lucent Books, 2002).

"Now I know I should have left my feelings...": Johnson, Earvin "Magic" with Roy S. Johnson. *Magic's Touch* (Reading, MA: Addison-Wesley Publishing Co., Inc., 1989).

"That blows my mind, knowing they...": Lazenby, Roland. *The Lakers: A Basketball Journey* (New York: St. Martin's Press, 1993).

"I know the game a lot better...": Grabowski, John. *The Los Angeles Lakers* (San Diego: Lucent Books, 2002).

"I think I played basically for an idea...": Abdul-Jabbar, Kareem and Mignon McCarthy. *Kareem* (New York: Random House, 1990).

Basketball Royalty

"I'm asked a lot what was the greatest thing...": Lazenby, Roland. *The Lakers: A Basketball Journey* (New York: St. Martin's Press, 1993).

Then Came Shaq

"Prior to last year I thought he was just...": Grabowski, John. *The Los Angeles Lakers* (San Diego: Lucent Books, 2002).

"No man can stop him, and you can't play a zone...": Grabowski, John. *The Los Angeles Lakers* (San Diego: Lucent Books, 2002).

WINNERS AND WHINERS
1968–69: Soap Opera
"He was upset by the trade...": Lazenby, Roland. *The Lakers: A Basketball Journey* (New York: St. Martin's Press, 1993).

A Fitting Match
"I didn't know how to lead people...": Grabowski, John. *The Los Angeles Lakers* (San Diego: Lucent Books, 2002).

THINGS TO SAVOR
Superstar
"I tell black players today, there was a guy...": Travers, Steven. *One Night, Two Teams, and the Game That Changed a Nation* (Lanham, MD: Taylor Trade Publishing, 2007).

"He never shot much unless...": Grabowski, John. *The Los Angeles Lakers* (San Diego: Lucent Books, 2002).

"It was just a typical Baylor performance...": Grabowski, John. *The Los Angeles Lakers* (San Diego: Lucent Books, 2002).

The Defining Moment
"Paul's fear was that we couldn't...": Lazenby, Roland. *The Lakers: A Basketball Journey* (New York: St. Martin's Press, 1993).

"The number one thing is desire...": Lazenby, Roland. *The Lakers: A Basketball Journey* (New York: St. Martin's Press, 1993).

"The way I look at my role as a floor leader...": Johnson, Earvin "Magic" with Roy S. Johnson. *Magic's Touch* (Reading, MA: Addison-Wesley Publishing Co., Inc., 1989).

NUMBERS DON'T LIE (OR DO THEY?)
33 Straight!
"I approached Wilt...": Travers, Steven. "33 Straight!" *StreetZebra*, November 1999.

Camelot and Figueroa

"But in Los Angeles, unlike Chicago...": Jackson, Phil. *The Last Season* (New York: The Penguin Press, 2004).

THE WRONG SIDE OF THE LAW

Hotel California

"Wilt was a powerful black man, a symbol to an entire race...": Abdul-Jabbar, Kareem and Peter Knobler. *Giant Steps: The Autobiography of Kareem Abdul-Jabbar* (New York: Bantam Books, 1983).

"You worried like hell...": Lazenby, Roland. *The Lakers: A Basketball Journey* (New York: St. Martin's Press, 1993).

"Jerry West was a brilliant young man...": Lazenby, Roland. *The Lakers: A Basketball Journey* (New York: St. Martin's Press, 1993).

The Punch

"He told me that in the ghetto you always...": Lazenby, Roland. *The Lakers: A Basketball Journey* (New York: St. Martin's Press, 1993).

Tark and the Murder Mystery

"...shady deals with Rams owner Carroll Rosenbloom...": Lazenby, Roland. *The Lakers: A Basketball Journey* (New York: St. Martin's Press, 1993).

SCANDAL

"I Cried When I Found Out."

"After every game, we'd have this entourage...": Lazenby, Roland. *The Lakers: A Basketball Journey* (New York: St. Martin's Press, 1993).

CELEBRITY CORNER

You Don't Know Jack

"I had to educate my players who the Celtics were...": Heisler, Mark. *The Lives of Riley* (New York: MacMillan, 1994).

There was one guy...": Lazenby, Roland. *The Lakers: A Basketball Journey* (New York: St. Martin's Press, 1993).